Hildegard of Bingen

Also by Colleen Keating and published by Ginninderra Press

A Call To Listen (Shortlisted, Society of Women Writers
NSW Book Awards 2016)
Fire on Water (Highly Commended, Society of Women Writers
NSW Book Awards 2018; Nautilus Award – Silver 2017)
Landscape of the Heart, with John Egan (Picaro Poets)

Colleen Keating

Hildegard of Bingen
A poetic journey

Acknowledgements

The poem 'A Feather on the Breath of God', adapted from the poem 'in search of Hildegard of Bingen', which was a finalist in the Dame Mary Gilmore Poetry Award for the 90th anniversary of the Society of Women Writers NSW 2016 (Giving Women a Voice), and several other poems in my second poetry collection *Fire on Water* inspire and inform this writing. The poem 'Viriditas' is adapted from my poem 'the smell of parsley' in my first poetry collection, *A Call to Listen*.

For their positive critique, affirmation and support, I would like to thank Pip Griffin and The Fellowship of Australian Writers,(Sydney); Sue Good (convenor) and the Women Writers Network; Norm Neill and fellow poets of the Wednesday Evening Poetry Group at NSW Writers Centre Rozelle. Thanks to Ron Wilkins and our U3A Poetry Appreciation Group (Epping) for their friendship.

Thank you to Pip Griffin, Decima Wraxall, Margaret Hede and Michael Keating for the final edits of this work.

My loving appreciation to Michael for his constant presence and inspiration.

For the poetry that is our children and their families.

Hildegard of Bingen: A poetic journey
ISBN 978 1 76041 766 6
Copyright © text Colleen Keating 2019
Cover: *Illumination H for Hildegard* by Tania Crossingham,
Mediaeval illuminator, heraldic artist and teacher
(www.tania-crossingham.com)

First published 2019 by
GINNINDERRA PRESS
PO Box 3461 Port Adelaide 5015
www.ginninderrapress.com.au

Contents

Foreword	9
Four Missionary Journeys of Hildegard of Bingen	11
Characters	12
Prologue: 1178	**15**
Defiance	17
Unruly Mystic	19
1: 1112–1120	**21**
Noble Women	23
Arrival	25
Becoming an Anchorite	27
The Anchorage	29
Jutta von Sponheim	31
Wide-eyed and Curious	33
Monastic Way	34
Confessor	35
Womanhood	37
Her Secret	38
Awakening World	40
Hildegard and the Young Man	42
II: 1120–1134	**45**
Getting of Knowledge	47
Intimacy	49
Anchorage to Convent	50
Richardis von Stade	52
A Healing Colour	54
Scriptorium	55
Epiphany	56
Feather on the Breath of God	57
Pilgrims	59

Viriditas	61
Her Secret Speaks	63

III: 1135–1137   65

Admonition	67
Separating of Ways	69
The Last Swallows	71
Passing of Jutta	73
Word Blooms	75
A Woman's Lot	76
Preparation for Burial	77
Standing her Ground	79

IV: 1138–1149   81

Counting Springs	83
A Call to Write	85
Abbot Kuno	87
First Writings	89
Letter to Bernard	91
Facing a Papal Envoy	93
Divine Revelation	95
Rule of Authority	97
Divine Command	99
Ending	102
Life or Death	104
Summonsed	105
Garnering Support	106

V: 1150–1152   109

Leaving Disibodenberg	111
Creating Rupertsberg	113
Dissent Emboldens Hildegard	115
Sense of Purpose	117
A New Earth	119

Cosmic Web	122
Unearthing Heaven	123
First Opera	125
The Art of Perseverance	126
Discernment	128
Anticipation	129
Touch of Silk	130
All Invited	132
Showcasing the Abbey	133
VI: 1152–1157	**135**
Disruption	137
Paralysis	139
Betrayed	141
Grief Comes Hard	143
Resilience	144
Renewed Fervour	147
Sister Clara	150
Fiery Light of Writing	152
Death of Richardis	155
Correspondence	158
Eleanor	160
Seer of Destiny	162
VII: 1158–1175	**165**
Three Missionary Journeys, 1158–1162	167
A Hum of Learning	170
Expansion to Eibingen	171
Volmar	173
Stand up for Freedom	175
The Letter	177
Release of Dowries	178
Ripening	179

Felicity	181
Last Missionary Journey	183
Passing of Volmar	185
An Obstinant Hierarchy	187

VIII: 1176–1178 — 189

Fidelity	191
Guibert of Gembloux	193
Hospitality	195
Summer	197
A Visit from the Canon of Mainz	198
Defiance	201
All is Well	203

IX: 1178–1179 — 205

Interdict	207
Without Song	209
Struggle in Exile	210
Endurance	212
My Quill, My Sabre	214
The Final Letter	216
The Long Silence	218
Her Last River Journey	219
Much Joy, Much Pain	222
Last Days	223
Hildegard's Song	225
A Circle Ends Where it Begins	226

Epilogue	229
Chronology	230
Glossary	235
Notes	241
Bibliography	246

Foreword

I fell in love with Hildegard of Bingen in 1996, when I read a book lent to me by a friend, who had studied at the School of Creative Spirituality in California. It was called *Illuminations of Hildegard of Bingen* (Matthew Fox, 1982) and was one of the first books about Hildegard translated into English. I was immediately drawn to know more about her. Hildegard quickly became an inspiring and wise companion.

To journey to Bingen on the Rhine River in Germany is a long trek for an Australian. It means swapping planes, trains, seasons, languages and cultures.

On my first visit to Bingen in the summer of 1998, I walked as a lone pilgrim in search of Hildegard. Standing in her Rhineland landscape, I found her, and have spent the last twenty years writing about my experience.

A second valuable visit to Bingen was in the autumn of 2014, with thirty Hildegard devotees from around the world led by pilgrim Abbess Christine Valters Paintner. For three weeks, we lived the Benedictine way – prayer, work, study – immersing ourselves in Hildegard's world. We spent time at her abbey singing the Divine Office, celebrating her feast day with the Benedictine Sisters who today model Hildegard's joy, laughter and hospitality.

My third visit to Hildegard's world was for a week in the spring of 2017, when my husband Michael and I walked in Hildegard's footsteps, familiarised ourselves with the Rhine River and the vineyards, and met guides and scholars, gleaning more portals into her world.

Out of the darkness and pain of her own journey, Hildegard

speaks. She sings and writes. She travels and preaches. Hildegard resists to the end, with courage, determination and at times defiance, against patriarchy, ignorance, superstition, fear and betrayal. She urges us to wake up, take responsibility, make choices. She stands for justice and mercy. She finds no room for fear, no excuse for silence. Her eighty-two years vibrate with so much creativity and expansion of consciousness that she calls us still over eight hundred years later, *to rise from our sleep* and *live with passion and blood* in order that we might contribute to enrich the turning of our cosmos with justice and compassion.

To commemorate my twenty-year anniversary, I present *Hildegard of Bingen: A Poetic Journey*.

Four Missionary Journeys of Hildegard of Bingen

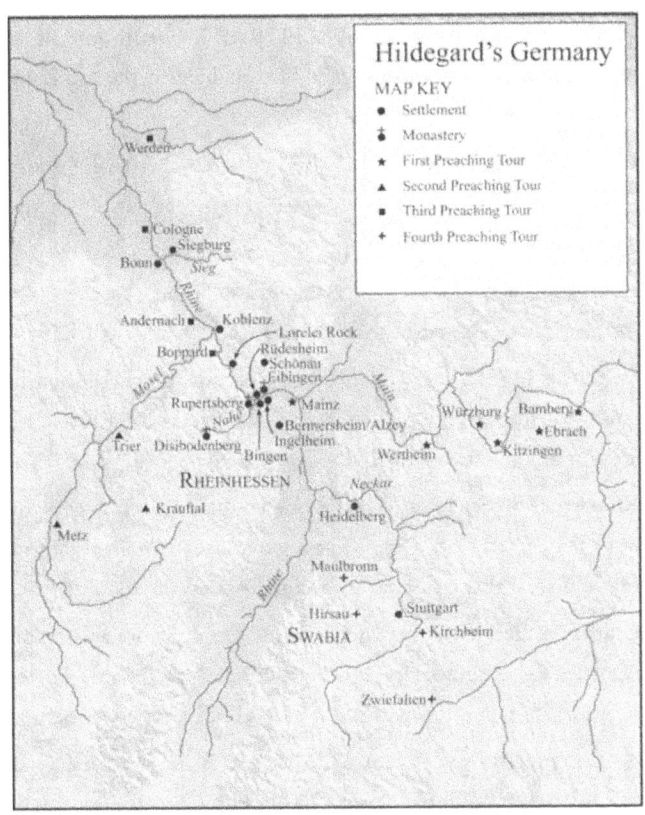

1159: first journey along the Main River to Bamberg
1160: second journey to Trier and Lorraine
1161: third journey down the Rhine to Siegburg and Cologne
1171: fourth journey through Swabi

Characters

Historical

Hildegard von Bingen 1098–1179: a German woman of extraordinary spirit and courage; she challenged the monastic and secular thinking of her time.

Jutta von Sponheim 1091–1136: a noblewoman who chose to become an anchoress; Hildegard was in her care from the age of eight.

Kuno: abbot of the monastery at Disibodenberg (about sixty monks); he established the anchorage and later the convent.

Volmar ?–1173: a scholarly monk at Disibodenberg; Hildegard's confessor; he became her secretary and scribed her visions; he accompanied her to Rupertsberg.

Richardis von Stade 1126–1152: joined the convent at age eight to be instructed by her Aunt Jutta; gifted friend and assistant to Hildegard; left Rupertsberg to become Abbess of Bassum.

Clara: a scholarly sister from a noble family, who set up the Apotheke at Rupertsberg and became Hildegard's aide in the scriptorium when Richardis left; next abbess at Rupertsberg.

Guda: entered the convent with her cousin Richardis; at first uneasy about the move from Disibodenberg to Rupertsberg; the vineyards and gardens thrived under her care.

Marchioness von Stade: wealthy patroness; mother of Richardis.

Bernard of Clairvaux 1090–1153: Cistercian abbot and mystic; he secured the acceptance of Hildegard's writings; friend and mentor to Pope Eugenius III.

Bishop Henry: Bishop of Mainz.

Eugenius III: Pope 1145–1153; at the Synod of Triers, 1147, he gave papal approval to Hildegard's writing.

Frederick Barbarossa 1122–1190: King of Germany and Holy Roman Emperor; he gave Hildegard's abbey a Decree of Imperial Protection; both abbeys would remain untouched.

Gottfried ?–1175: monk; replaced Volmar as priest and Hildegard's secretary in 1174.

Guibert of Gembloux: Latin scholar from the Monastery of Gembloux in Belgium; served as priest and secretary to Hildegard 1176–79.

Helengerus: abbot; Kuno's successor at Disibodenberg.

Clementia ?–1177: Hildegard's older sister; widow; came to join Hildegard and provided special comfort.

Christian: Archbishop of Mainz; chancellor to Barbarossa; served the interdict against Hildegard.

Fictional

Inez: an aristocratic woman and self taught scholar; prepares medicines and assists in infirmary, fluent in Latin and is able to tutor the sisters in Latin; accompanies Hildegard on her first pilgrimage to confront Barbarossa; chosen as the magistra for the new abbey at Eibingen.

Odelia: from a farming family near Bremen; loves the outdoors; cares for the grapevines but her special craft is beekeeping.

Wilfredis: widow; comes to Disibodenberg and experiences the move to Rupertsberg with Hildegard; initially disappointed but later very supportive; assists Clara in the apotheke and infirmary and takes over when Clara moves to the scriptorium; highly organised.

Bertrude and Agnes: sisters from the south, trained as seamstresses; their dowries included reams of silk; they sew vestments and altar cloths for the abbey and also on commission.

Prologue
1178

Defiance

Hildegard tucks up her coarse tunic,
leans heavily on her staff,
struggles down
onto rough cemetery ground
by the orchard trees.
Her eighty-one-year-old bones
tremble, fire with rage.

She kneels on tilled earth,
heaves at a wooden cross.

Her frail determined body
rocks it, forwards, backwards.

It takes all her strength,
a tug of war with herself and the earth,
a war with the bishop and priests of Mainz.

Dawn will bring an inquisition.
Soldiers charged to exhume a body,
ordered to burn the remains.

Hildegard must disguise this burial site.
The young sisters cannot be asked to help.
This is her doing.

She wrenches it out,
still on her knees, holds it high
against a dark louring sky
defiant.

Breathless,
she pulls out another and another,
falls into the mud,
her face buried in mired crosses.

She edges herself up.
Hugs a cross,
her arms holding herself together.

Alone in this darkly light,
lost in murmurs
of the Rhine River below,
she treads cold, tired steps
into the nightmare of her choice.

Unruly Mystic

Word reaches the archbishop of Mainz,
mutters around his court.
Hildegard defies the order to exhume
the body of a *heretic*, blessed
then buried in her consecrated ground.

The army returns,
embarrassed, red-faced.
They could not carry out their orders,
the burial plot could not be found.

Archbishop Arnold blusters.
He jumps to his feet.
Rustle of his red silk and lace robe
lost in his anger.
The ruby ring on his pudgy finger flashes.

This so-called holy lady will not win this battle,
her wilful disobedience must be punished.
He bangs his fist onto the podium.
The clerics jump in fear.
The excommunicated
will not be buried in consecrated land.
This unruly so-called mystic will not get away with this.
He points to the canon:
Ride and carry these words,

he dips his quill in ink,
scratches at the parchment
with seismic jolts
press of ruby ring into seal wax.

I place an interdict on her abbeys.
Isolation, no sacraments.
Her music is forbidden.
Make her suffer.

1
1112–1120

As the seed planted deeply dies, so too do I die
— John 12:24

Noble Women

Anno Domini November 1112
The Rhineland moon
edges the icy road,
lights an entourage
of uniformed men
servants, local peasants.

Hildegard sits strong-backed
on a young spirited horse.
All fourteen years of her
bubbles with questions.

Besides her chatter
and dawn-crackle of ice,
there is a shuffle of carts
overburdened with dowries,
erratic shivers of the horses
with huff of dragon smoke.

How long is our journey? she asks.

Jutta in a noble gown and veil
yearning for her new monastic life
rides a smooth-gaited palfrey,
says softly,
*we will be there by noon
in time to prepare for our ceremony.*

Will the monks be happy to receive us?
Hildegard muses, proud to accompany
this beautiful woman, her teacher.

*Of course. Our families have donated.
The monastery has prepared
our own anchorage,
built adjoining their chapel.
Together we can die to this world
to be only brides for Christ.*

Arrival

Disibodenberg, high in the forest
sprawls in the clouds.
The last mile steeply uphill.
Secluded.

A white butterfly dips and lifts.
Hildegard's gaze follows it up
catches the glint of the sun
on the first stone wall.

Stoic buildings unfold
cloistered around a cobbled garth.
Their Benedictine monastery.

A monk in cinctured black robe
walks from the signposted infirmary.
From beneath his blinkered cowl
he extends a welcome.
They dismount.
Jutta falls on her knees in gratitude.

Hildegard overjoyed, breathes
the space of leafless beech and elms
in the skinniness of winter.
White-tipped branches
disguise trees of apple and pear.
Grapevines cling bare along stone walls.

Frosty breath hangs in the air.
Her new home,
a frisson of gold in the cool noon sun.

The ring of hammer and anvil,
chink of chisel, thwack of axe,
clank of well come to a hush
as a bell tolls. To the shuffle
and hiss of sandals,
forty robed monks file to chapel.

Hearing a deep, rich chant
Hildegard looks up
as it resonates with her.

Becoming an Anchorite

Is it the bite
of cold stone
that makes Hildegard shiver?

This, the chosen day of vows,
Feast of All Saints.
Liminal moment,
between natural and supernatural,
membrane thin.

Monks and pilgrims gather,
crowded faces flicker
in the chapel candlelight.
Their chant intones the funeral dirge.
Words fill the air, heavy, dark.
Swing of thurible
wafts the woody aroma of incense.

Jutta and Hildegard
lie prone on the ground,
arms outstretched.
Dying to self,
their *calvary*,
crossed with burnt tree ash.
Their sacrifice,
their offering.

Hildegard smells scattered dust,
feels it sprinkled on her back.
A dank chill
seeps into her bones.

No comfort in Jutta's voice.
Lying prostrate next to her
Jutta laments, under her black veil,
death desires me and I accept,
here I will stay forever as chosen.

Stepping into the dark
with flame-lit procession,
and crunch of leaves,
they enter the new anchorage.

Dank straw assaults Hildegard's breath,
blackness stretches all around,
deathly, cold.

Jutta places her candle on a stone altar
kindles the small set fire in the hearth,
kneels and prays.
Hildegard beside her,
shrouded by gloom, whispers,
as the seed planted deeply
dies to itself
so too do I die.

Her heart pounds
with hammer blows,
as nails assault the wooden door.

They are walled in,
entombed.

The Anchorage

A bell startles the dark.
Hildegard wakes.
How cold she is
gripped in the fist of night,
viced with fear, and stale air.
Her pallet of straw, no comfort.

Shadow of Jutta already on her knees.
Hildegard follows.

Candlelight flickers
through a squint on the far wall.
Male voices chant into the dawn.

The slant of day
softens harshness of stone,
exposes to her stunned eyes
her confinement.
Altar, rude wooden table, stools,
wax tablet, stylus.
Iron cooking bowls wait
near a hearth's dying embers.
On a stone ledge
stands Jutta's stringed psaltery,
her psalter and breviary
bound in deer hide.

A narrow high-walled patch of earth,
bucket of water, garden spade,
stacked wood.

After matins and prime
Jutta rekindles the fire,
rubs her warmed hands
into the knot of her back.

Hildegard watches Jutta
push back a black curtain
open a wooden fly-window.
She smells the earthy aroma
of spelt bread.
Jutta receives it silently from a monk
and they cook their first meal,
pottage and boiled cabbage.

Jutta von Sponheim

Word spreads about *Blessed Jutta*,
the anchorite at Disibodenberg,
one who turned away well marked suitors,
spurned love of men for love of God.

Many, especially women, seek her counsel,
her healing and blessing.

In her twentieth year,
Jutta has found her home.
Her calling burns in her heart,
fires her soul.

Wealthy, ambitious, headstrong,
her dowry, her influence.

Even before terce, they queue
with market-day commotion,
from local hamlets below,
pilgrims from afar,
gifts and food for the monks
some with livestock, produce from their gardens.

Jutta sits at the black-veiled window,
listens, offers benediction.

She covets sainthood.
Her ethereal white skin,
her sage holiness
shines before her confessor, Abbot Kuno.

In his decision to build this anchorage
and welcome *this future saint*
he sees revenue for his monastery,
and a planned place of pilgrimage.

Wide-eyed and Curious

Under Jutta's tutelage,
Hildegard writes out prayers.
Wide-eyed and curious
she absorbs the Divine Office.
With the tablet and stylus
Latin comes alive.

The ten strings of the psaltery
zither the air
as she sings the psalms.
She and Jutta stitch gifted fine silk
for altar cloths and vestments.

Stone walls, monastic chant
by osmosis, her world of music.
Sometimes her mind drifts back to home,
smell of the Bermersheim forest
and meadows in spring.
How she loved running wildly
that last summer
in the woods with her brother Roerich.

In moments of loneliness
she glances inwards.
Was she a *tithe* to God
the last of ten children?
Or despite a mother's warning
was she betrayed
by her *secret*?

Monastic Way

Cold dissipates
like fog in morning light.
The fullness of summer is upon Hildegard.
For the first time in months
her body breathes easily.

Prayer envelops her in love,
quietens her heart.
She rests
in the arms of entombing walls
and Benedictine rhythm,
prayer, work, study.

Pastel colours of rising and setting suns,
moonlight shadows on courtyard wall
wax and wane
seasons, smells and sounds
release, ripen,
cycles ground her.

In the absence of the world
and in her isolation,
she finds presence.
Every sense comes to bud
blossoms alive
opens with soft sighs of delight.

She loves the dart of the swallows
nested under the church eave,
the intoxicating smell of each hour,
even the clang of the bell sings to her.

Confessor

Abbot Kuno, Hildegard's confessor
bites with authority.
Let go of the senses,
they are not to be trusted,
the monastic way calls for you
to cultivate the inner world.
Be more like Jutta, follow her ways
if you want to be half the woman she is.

He questions Hildegard's sincerity,
annoyed by her fervour.
He knows he is not the confessor for her.
Blessed Jutta is different
he tells himself impatiently,
compliant and so very holy.
A saint in the making.

Hildegard hears his deep gravelly voice
through the black-curtained window,
feels his impervious edge as he states,
You leave yourself open
to the devil's temptation.

Hildegard's senses are not validated.
Aroma of seasons, dart of birds,
her tiny pocket of cloud and sky,
all that inspires her love of creation
from her stoned-in anchorage is denied.

Sometimes when breeze plays the curtain
her eyes dance.
Images of nature slip inside
move through her limbs, murmur their truth
deep into her heart.
She notices her toes tapping.
Yet during the day
whenever she looks at the black curtain
from where his voice had come
Hildegard is reminded
worthless to the world.

Womanhood

In her womanhood,
blood flows.
She counts
dark moon to dark moon,
season to season.
Her rhythm,
the rhythm of mother earth.

Resilient after snow, a rose bud
belies the confined courtyard
and the winter that cloaks its life.

Jutta commissions a hair shirt,
a sign Hildegard has come of age.
Hildegard rejects it
with lightening sparks of defiance
her voice a knapper's screech of flint.
Jutta steps back in shock
watching Hildegard flame.

As mentor, Jutta
admires this spark of defiance.
She will stoke its fiery passion
with parchments
she requests from the monks' library.
Enliven Hildegard's curiosity
embolden her thirst to learn.

Even as Hildegard refuses
she blossoms from the love
mirrored in Jutta's eyes.

Her Secret

Hildegard
takes her vows, a professed nun.
Prostrate before the bishop,
he reminds her:
you are in the shadow
and you choose to live a life
of submission and humility.
He sprinkles holy water on her back,
she breathes resin of incense-puffed air,
hears the chain-clink
as the thurible swings over her.

My choice, Hildegard whispers in her heart.

She remembers the fear in her mother's eyes
when she visioned the unseen,
when she told her brothers and sisters
the colour of an unborn calf,
when a beautiful light spoke to her,
when she knew more than she should
when her mother warned her to remain silent,
for fear it is the devil at work.
Walled-in, she can hide.
Let them be, let them die,
devote myself to God,
die to myself,
forever.

Hildegard's years pass
with fealty to silence.
Jutta keeps her confidence.

Often the Light calls to Hildegard
strikes her down, blinds her,
refuses to leave for days.
Lying in dark silence,
her straw pallet is her refuge.

Awakening World

Jutta kneels in prayer.
Hildegard quietly
moves over to the window,

shifts the black curtain
ever so slightly.
Spring breeze teases her face.
The coo of nearby doves
a distant cuckoo,
scent of blossoms
from an awakening world.

In that patch of sky,
she sees freedom,
as swallows sally and skim
to a nest of mud and stick,
above the courtyard under the turret.

*Ah! how I long for the moist lushness
and greenness of fields.*

Her throat tenses.
Her breath quickens.
The thick stone walls oppress her.
She hears a voice within,
Trust me, trust me.

The squint on the other side beckons.
She eases over, kneels,
glances into the chapel
as she does to receive the sacrament
from Abbot Kuno.

Hildegard sees a young man,
hood of his cowl thrown back,
immersed in a warm glow of altar light.

Hildegard and the Young Man

Magic of seeds.
Hildegard digs the patch of earth
in their tiny high-walled courtyard.
She plans a bounty of culinary herbs
in this pocket of fresh air
sky, clouds, birds.

Tapping at the window
breaks Hildegard's reverie.

Little sister, can you hear me?

Through the gentle swell of the curtain,
the afternoon sun
haloes the young man from the chapel.

Here little sister,
some herbs,
from the forest,
for your courtyard.

He passes them through.

She feels the warmth of his hand.
The fresh moist smell of the forest
jolts her back to days of freedom.

My name is Volmar.
I am to replace Abbot Kuno
as your confessor.
I am a scribe in the scriptorium.

Scriptorium?

Yes, it is a large, light room.
We scrutinise and copy
scrolls and manuscripts.

I bring books for Jutta.
Now I will bring them for you.

As he walks away,
a sparrow alights
on the high stone wall,
turns its head from side to side,
looks hard at a piece of mortar,
pecks at it,
flies away.
A brisk whirring of wings.
Hildegard smiles.

II
1120–1134

Getting of Knowledge

Seasons fall one upon another.
Hildegard tends their courtyard,
a patchwork of green colour.

Pilgrims throng to Disibodenberg,
seek Jutta for blessing.
Jutta sits at her window
to the world.
Hildegard observes Jutta's gifts
of healing and prophecy,
aware of the pilgrims, their fears,
their sense of longing.

After Divine Office
the monk Volmar taps the window,
gives them a vellum-bound manuscript.
He speaks softly,
This is my new work.

In dim afternoon light
Hildegard and Jutta sit together,
marvel at illuminated works
he has copied into German
of the vegetation sheltered
in woodlands and meadows,
herbs, ferns, moss and lichen.

They pore over each page.
Illuminations shimmer
under Hildegard's enquiring gaze.
They smell the hide, minerals,
ink's oak oil, plant dye.
Hildegard's hunger quickens.
Her hunger for the *getting of knowledge*.

Intimacy

Seasons fold one to the other,
sixteen years of seasons,
smells of spring and summer,
frozen courtyard of winter.
Rhythm of prayer and music
biblical words, monks chant,
and their readings sustain them.

Jutta and Hildegard,
close as mother and daughter,
give their mornings to pilgrims.
Afternoons, in joyous spirit
nimble fingers embroider altar robes
for the Bishop of Mainz.
Today, sewing a fine damask rose silk,
heads down
as close as two birds at a feeding tray.

At vesper bell, both stand
reach out, embrace,
breathing synchronised.
Time beats slower
a profound moment of silence
in the knowing of deep friendship.

Anchorage to Convent

Outside the anchorage
chisel on stone,
hammer on nail,
masons, carpenters, artisans.
Hildegard listens to each sweet sound,
taps her fingers
to this music of freedom.

They are to be a convent,
no longer closed in an anchorage.
Three postulants will arrive,
Jutta's nieces, Richardis,
Adelheid and Guda.
Others aspire to join.
Their dowries,
Abbot Kuno couldn't resist.

After twenty years
change breathes into their world.
After twenty years of being walled in,
Hildegard has not forgotten
the fresh, green, lush world,
the sky, blue as the wild hyacinths
of her childhood.
She rubs her hands together,
excited with the feeling of freedom.
She visualises paradise of gardens,
inhales their aromas, drinks in colour.

Her eyes sparkle pride
as they are made a convent
and Jutta is blessed as Magistra
acclaimed holy,
her sainthood assured.

Jutta holds to her enclosure,
My vow of stability is here.
But for Hildegard her walled-in world
bursts like the acorn,
and she, like its seed
blows free on the wind.

Her time has come.

Her body knows what she wants,
she can almost taste her opportunity
as honey birds know
the most succulent flower,
and geese instinctively migrate.

Richardis von Stade

Cavalry in red uniforms.
Standard bearers of the House of Stade.
Flags flutter, peasants, stock, carts of goods,
hoofbeats, horn calls.
The brilliance of a noble entourage.

The Marchioness von Stade arrives
richly attired, proudly mounted
on her dark chestnut palfrey
accompanied by her own vassals.
Monks bow to her
Abbot Kuno hurries out, fusses
as he receives her daughter, Richardis.

Richardis, an excited eight-year-old
is given into her holy Aunt Jutta's care.
Her dark sapphire eyes
sparkling with stars,
regard Hildegard with anticipation.

Hildegard is reminded of herself
curious, eager to learn.

Richardis quickly follows Hildegard,
learns to read, write, draw.
Her slender fingers
run across the strings of the psaltery.
Music draws them together.

Seasons pass.

Marchioness von Stade often visits.
Abbot Kuno entertains her.

She bears gifts of lands,
a fief, a new toll gate, livestock,
silken cloth for vestments,
parchment, goose feathers,
lapis lazuli and gold leaf for the scriptorium.

She spends little time with her daughter,
yet is assured the convent runs smoothly.

A Healing Colour

The none bell fills the air
for afternoon prayer.
Richardis runs ahead with the sisters.
Hildegard in their new garden
lingers a moment, cherishing the freedom.
Her basket filled.
She gazes around her
sighs with joy.
Her smile can hardly be contained.
How she relishes these moments
to be lost in the loving, living Light.

Dappled, the sun
textures trees and grasses,
with crunch of heaping leaves underfoot,
a riot of russet and gold.

Affirmation comes on the breeze,
God hugs you.
You are encircled by the arms
of the mystery of God.
Feast your eyes on the green
a thousand shades of green
a healing colour, let it heal you
with its greening power, rooted in the sun.[1]

This moment is my miracle
she murmurs,
as she hastens back to the convent.

Scriptorium

Maybe it is the light
that illuminates jars
of coloured minerals, powders.

Maybe the smell of curing skin,
or sharp tang of vinegar.
It could be the plaited basket
of moss and flower, blue woad dye
or sharp smell of ink
pestled down from bald-oak.

Maybe the sight of scrolls
rolled into alcoves
or shelved parchments,
or the elaborate books of saints
behind the monk Volmar
enshrined on the *cumdach*.

Perhaps it's the copy of Ptolemy's *Astronomy*,
or the manuscripts
Volmar points out,
from all over the Christian and Arab world.

Maybe just crossing the threshold
when Hildegard steps through the door,
inhales the air
and feels immediately at home
in a world that sharpens curiosity.

Hildegard knows,
she has found her calling.
She wants to be a maker of books.

Epiphany

In the garden, Hildegard sings
of soft hills
curved as a mother's breast,
The earth is at the same time mother,
She is mother of all that is natural,
mother of all that is human.
She is the mother of all,
for contained in her
are the seeds of all.[2]

She sings of trees and plants
ferns, herbs, flowers and stones.
The greening power of God's love
surges through her
palpable holiness of vitality.

Hildegard learns
names of the plants, herbs
their healing properties.
The sisters' garden explodes
a paintbox come to life
spilling across a landscape.

Richardis follows her,
discerns culinary and medicinal plants,
bubbles intensely,
alive with the world.

Feather on the Breath of God

The barn swallows swoop and call
busy at work under the chapel turret.
Hildegard muses how when frost arrives
they fly off
for warmer climes.
Now they have returned.

With light-hearted skip
she races in from the garden
to share her joy with Jutta.

Her face lit with the warmth of the sun,
bonnet and wimple in hand.
Long blousy russet skirt
tucked into a rope cincture around her waist,
stockings and thick tan sandals
exposed.

Jutta, O Jutta
she calls
it is so beautiful.
I see the Light and beyond to the heavens
not as in ecstasy but with my eyes wide open
I want to express myself so much,
I feel so blessed.[3]

She plucks a feather
from under her coarse, homespun cape,
and look, a gift.
I know there are always feathers,
but this was special, as I watched it drift.
I felt a 'yes' to life.
Ah, I am a feather on the breath of God.[4]
She turns both hands in the air,
eyes to the heavens,
a twirl of gratitude,
a dance of light.

Wiry body bent over a loom
Jutta looks up,
her eyes smile lovingly.
Then comes her clear strong voice
like a crash of an earthenware jar.
Hildegard is brought back to earth,
grounded as the rich alluvial mud
from the herb garden
stuck all over her sandals.

My child, hush, that is enough.
Jutta says firmly
Do you have the herbs from the garden?
They need to be prepared for the tonics.
We need more violets and aloe for salve
for the sick tomorrow.
Gather the sisters to help you,
and wood, for tomorrow's meal,
needs to be split before vespers.

Pilgrims

Blessed Jutta is not well.
It is she, Hildegard,
who will listen, advise, counsel.

At the infirmary
it is she, Hildegard,
who welcomes lines of pilgrims
waiting for Jutta
– many from nearby hamlets,
some from afar.

After matins the monks call
for her assistance.
This day, a young child ails
with fever.
Hildegard prepares hot and cold compresses
makes a poultice of balsam and pressed-oil salve.
The monks watch and listen.

Hildegard's growing fame
confuses Abbot Kuno.

Many now call her name
as humanity exposes itself,
in misery, smell of poverty,
fearful, ignorant.

Hildegard cares especially for the women,
powerless in their control,
who bleed monthly,
give birth too many times,
whose bent bodies cramp,
and overheat in age.

It is the monk, Volmar
who scouts out books
for Hildegard's healing knowledge.

Hildegard teaches the sisters,
now grown to ten, busy
in the Benedictine rhythm.
Jutta still weak, looks on with pride.

Like a deer to its mother
Richardis looks to Hildegard.
The sisters move around the monastery,
support the monks. Guda helps
with the vineyard.
They enlarge the garden,
help the monks
in the infirmary, scriptorium.

Abbot Kuno builds
a small oratory for his sisters,
alert to their fame and charisma
and the revenue
they attract to his monastery.

Viriditas

After the rains
Hildegard tends the garden
knee-deep
in wet grass,
up to her elbows in soil,
worms, snails
and ruff of leaf compost.

Marvels at the ramble
of a young squash vine,
a stray seed gone free.

Lingers in the fragrance
of chives and basil,
coriander, lavender and mint,
and the smell of parsley.

Savours their bouquet.
Being jubilant
with the flirt of white moths,
and the canticle of birdsong
from an oak branch above.
Dwells on her knees
as if in prayer.

Hildegard stands
her hands on her lower back
stretches and arches
skywards. Wisping clouds
ruffle. Light whispers,
I am the breeze that nurtures all things green
I encourage blossoms to flourish with ripening fruits
I am the rain coming from the dew
that causes the grasses to laugh
with the joy of life.[5]

Fearful of her own mystery
she clams shut this Light
into the tight knot of her gut.

Her Secret Speaks

Hildegard's visions of the radiant Light
will not be silenced.
Its life force
grows brighter.

Hildegard confesses,
Words move in me, a blaze of true and Living Light.
It calls me. I hear it say,
write down that which you see and hear.[6]

Jutta fears for her.
It must be kept secret.
She warns silence.

Only Volmar, your confessor
must know.
Heresy is dangerous, keep your counsel.
A seer is accused of devil mingling,
excommunicated.
For a woman this means death.

Hildegard seeks her sick bed.
Days of headache
unseeing eyes,
flashing whiteness, spin of black space,
she wakes to Jutta's care.
Drained.
Spent.

III
1135–1137

Admonition

Jutta sits in silent prayer,
her hand on the book of psalms
which she now never has to open.
Twenty-four years of repetition,
the prayers say themselves,
she once said.

Hildegard chooses an apple
from the freshly picked load,
last of the season.
Slices it thin as parchment,
inhales its crisp juiciness
carries it into Jutta's dim cell.

She smacks the wooden bowl down.
Jutta looks up.
A line-drawn face haggers her,
anchored here in fetid air.

Hildegard frowns as she ponders
If the pilgrims saw Jutta now
they would question her way.

Wrapping her closely in the rug,
Hildegard checks the chilblains
from Jutta's barefoot walks
in the frosted courtyard,
admonishes this penance,
groans more with anger than pity.
Jutta's feet are beyond the salve
of her peppercorn balm.

You will die, Jutta.
Remember
from Volmar's parched scrolls we read
the Hippocratic oath,
'I will keep pure and holy my life and my art,
compassion for each other,'
Hildegard whispers despairingly,
'but also for myself'[7]
She raises her voice, continues with anguish,
In my visions with the Divine Light
it speaks of the body as a sacred temple,
a sanctuary to radiate God's magnificence.

She holds Jutta's gaze.
Do not be captured by the devil.
Our body is one with the soul.
You stifle that unity.

Hildegard's hands are clenched
as she turns and exits.

Separating of Ways

Something aggressive
in the way Hildegard enters
Jutta's cell in the old anchorage.

Jutta lies on her straw bed,
life drained,
her eyes stone-grey.

Her feeble, caved shoulders
once broad and strong,
jolt Hildegard.
She can no longer stay silent.
She shakes with anger.
In a curious paradox,
she has been indecisive.
Until now.

Jutta grimaces,
starved, flagellated.
Her hair-shirted body
cries its sacrifice.

Hildegard sits, takes her hand,
notices its translucent skin
transfigured
in her triumph of soul
to find sainthood.
Hildegard sighs.

Like a fish
lost in the ocean
in search of the ocean,
Jutta is lost in holiness
in search of it.

A chill shivers the air.
From a sparse stillness
winter wind violently
bangs the door shut
– a turning point.
Hildegard sees beyond harsh ascetics
even as she dearly loves her sister.

The Last Swallows

Hildegard's world stands bleak,
bare. The last swallows long gone.
In cold light
dewdrops hang on a blade of grass.
Lingering dread
knots her stomach.

She enters the anchorage
sighs deeply,
lights Advent's second candle.
Smoky glow reveals
the pale beauty of Jutta's face.
She lies stilled.
Hildegard puts down some bowls,
kisses her forehead.

Jutta, my mother,
your ascetics are too harsh.
Your imprisoned cell here
is mortification enough.

Let our spirits give praise
with rhythm of music,
with song of jubilation.
Our God, the Just One, is she who offers life
with all its bountiful gifts.[8]

She nurtures Jutta,
urges with sips of fennel tea,
warmed broth, mulled honeyed wine.
Oil from the olives, freshly pressed,
she heats over the smouldering hearth,
gently massages Jutta's hands and feet.
Her flesh wasted.

Jutta has her mind only
on heaven,
to be remembered as a saint.
Hildegard kneels beside her
holds her cold hands,
listens to her trailing breath.
She loves this broken woman.

Passing of Jutta

Teardrops of ice frame
the darkest evening of the year.
third week of Advent 1136.

Jutta is forty-four.
Her gaunt body
curled foetal on her straw palette,
with bony hands held in prayer,
she murmurs,
*my bridegroom died in pain for me,
and I die in pain, for Him to take me home.*

Hildegard knows the smell of death.

The sisters gather,
hear the last breaths,
as the lover of Christ,
walks the valley of death.
Richardis' young frightened eyes
stare down at her aunt.
Her hand clings to Hildegard.

Monks gather in the cobbled yard.
The light of early morning hints
not only an end but a beginning.

Jutta mumbles a litany of virgins and martyrs
Ursula, Barbara, Agatha.
Hildegard cries names
of strong biblical women
Deborah, Judith, Miriam, Esther, Ruth.

Powerless,
Hildegard bows her head,
releases the limp blue hand.
The candles gasp for air,
even the wax falls like tears.
She looks up
sees chilled faces of her ten sisters.
Their fear-filled eyes on her
their new magistra.

Word Blooms

Hildegard sighs deeply,
Her world shattered.[9]
My mother, my sister.
she cries as her body slumps.
From the stillness
she hears the stifled sobs
of her sisters
huddled in the cold stone corner.

Her body stiffens,
shakes.
Again her hands clench.
Anger rises.
Reason rips at her woman's body
I am life, it whispers,
I am life, whole and entire
all life has its roots in me.[10]
Vision of the Divine Light
shimmers in her mind
with its unified cosmos.

The Word blooms from her,
Blackness of night will never again
overcome the star-studded sky,[11]
she breathes defiantly.

Monks outside,
their chant fallen to silence,
wait.

A Woman's Lot

Golden in low winter dawn,
Hildegard walks out to the monks.
She stands bereft, alone.
Her composure razed to the bone.

Air hangs
silent, cold around her.
Speechless
she nods her head,
affirms Jutta's passing.

The Abbot and monks,
hard-faced,
turn their backs.
She is invisible.
They will plan the funeral.

A bitter wind
hits her
drills into her gut
bores into her mind.

Leather sandals,
even woollen stockings,
cannot prevent the bite of snow
that chills her spirit.

Entombed in loneliness,
her world shrouded
by helpless fragility

Preparation for Burial

The novices and sisters in her care
she busies with chores,
demands to be alone
to prepare Jutta for burial.

Hildegard washes the naked,
wasted body,
finds a putrid chain,
metal sharp in her flesh.

As if Jutta can still hear
Hildegard laments aloud,
Extremes lead to this.
There must be change.
There must be renewal.
The Church, the people must know,
a holistic way.

Fiery rage melds
like wax into compassion.
She dips the sponge in lavender water.
Washes.
She traces the lines on Jutta's face.
Remembering.

With scented oils and prepared herbs,
dried lavender, rose petals
saved from last season,
she whispers
as she wraps the body for burial,
I prepare you my Mother,
as your joyful daughter
to look on the Living God.
She gazes at the candle
it flickers in response.

Not looking back, she opens the door
steps into a cold draught.

A solitary figure,
she strides out to face Abbot Kuno.
Her step precise, even, determined
against winter wind and bracing cold.
Dead leaves, slippery as ice, pave her way.

Standing her Ground

Abbot Kuno's thunderous face
threatens flint-sharp.
No welcome.

Hildegard bows,
eyes downcast.
She cannot still the quiver in her voice
as she stutters out,
Your wretched servant
heartbroken creature
in God's sight as I am,
in the inferior form of a woman
beg for you to hear me.

She marshals her strength
comes to her full height
stands firmly grounded.
Her words bite the air,
air that hangs heavy over the room.

It is the stubborn man who refuses to change.
Hear the Lord in humility.

He steps back.
She gathers herself
stands tall,
wonders if he can sense her rapid breath.
Her spirit
soars like an eagle into the sun,
wings drip light.
She holds him with her sabre eyes.

My sisters will process into the Chapel
for Jutta's funeral,
with the bishop and monks.
We will sing a hymn I have composed.
We will not be silent,
we will be heard.
We will live.
My sisters will be invisible no more.

His face snaps
at her voice of command.
She has a new stance,
her bearing patrician.
Her eyes light up a bursting heart
as she turns away.

IV
1138–1149

O Virtus Sapientiae:
O moving force of Wisdom,
encircling the wheel of the cosmos.
Encompassing all that is,
all that has life,
in one vast circle...[12]

Counting Springs

The flirt of swallows
catches her eye.
A third spring since Jutta's passing.
Their blue feathers flicker
as they circle the splurge of stick and mud
high in the chapel wall.

She imagines their journey
buffeted by winds
lost and found,
plotting their way
slap of the sun by day
pin prick of stars by night.

Pilgrims flock for her counsel.
Several come to join her sisters.
Attentive, they wait upon her every word.

During Divine office
she listens enraptured
by her sisters singing the psalms
as she has taught them.

Richardis plucks the psaltery
looks over, smiles.
Hildegard's eyes widen,
she breathes deeply
sees not a young girl
but a beautiful woman.

Melancholy weighs her,
the potential of her sisters,
blocked, in a stagnant backwater
here at this monk's monastery.
Their future demands her struggle.
How many springs must pass?

A Call to Write

Hildegard leans
against the well's cold stone,
mutters a lament,
holds her aching head.

Help me. Give me strength.
Help me stand firm.
I don't know what to do.
Where should I turn? I am afraid.

Taut white winds
whip her words
an echo from the well.
A face etched darkly
mirrors from the deep,
framed in white coif and black veil.
Her fortieth year almost complete.

Light blinds her.
She hears the hum and strike of words:
O fragile human, ashes of ashes,
dust of dust,
say and write what you see and hear.[13]

Dizzy with revelation,
she huddles down
into the side of the well.

An anxious Volmar finds her,
carries her inside.

Richardis steadies her,
calls for warm broth
creamed in goat's milk.

The sisters care for her
heavy with the fear
of losing their magistra.
Ricardis's constancy,
love and reassurance
brings her back.

Abbot Kuno

Broad shoulders
heavy black serge tunic –
formidable as a stone wall.
His custom is to busy himself,
turn his back
when Hildegard appears.
Any benevolence died with Jutta.
He grieves her loss.

Pale, weak
Hildegard seeks an audience.
With daring she faces him.
He stares her down.

Stung by his look
her voice trembles.
She seeks permission to write.
A husky hint of tears.

Abbot Kuno paces,
hesitates, makes her wait.
Hildegard's neck muscles tighten,
her body shakes.

Afraid she will return to her sickbed
he clasps his pudgy hands, nods his head
thinks aloud,
snaps,
You will write.
Volmar, your confessor
will scribe these words you say you hear.
I will consult your future
with the bishop, Henry.

With a voice of ice he adds,
We do not want talk of heresy here.
We do not want shame brought
upon our Monastery.

He opens the Bible, glares,
Remember the words I have already read,
I suffer not a woman to teach,
nor usurp authority over man,
but to be in silence.[14]

First Writings

Hildegard's world shifts.
I feel awake, Volmar
I can write what I see, what I hear.
And you my scribe.

A sense of elation
swells through the scriptorium.
Volmar prepares a quire of parchment,
enough for two eight-page manuscripts.
He sits at the carved wood carrel,
waits, quill poised.

Hildegard waits, her mind battles.
Bullies of fear and humiliation
crowd in,
darkness stalks within her.

And then the Light shines through.
Her visions unfold,
her words gain wings, soar,
eagle-like into the sun.[15]

It is 1141.
Harvest is finished.

Her first book *Scivias* begins,
When I was forty-two years and seven months old
Heaven was opened,
and a fiery light of exceeding brilliance
came and permeated my whole mind,
inflamed my heart
and my breast,
not like a burning,
but a warming flame,
as the sun warms anything its rays touch.
And I heard the Light
who sits on the throne, speak.[16]

Her dictation is forthright
Volmar writes in Latin
Richardis by her side
listens to illumine her words.

Letter to Bernard

Five years of fruitful harvests,
busyness of bees in the orchard,
of voluptuous aromas,
grapes ferment,
and dewdrop on apples
dance a sparkle of light.

Volmar scribes Hildegard's visions
filling quires of parchment.

Abbot Kuno erodes her every move
to share her writings,
even with her sisters.

She thinks of the geese
their wings clipped,
earthbound in the field
against their nature.

What are these promptings
that feather-touch my heart?
How to envisage a future?

An idea whispers in her mind.
Hildegard recalls a vision
she didn't understand,
a man soars
like an eagle to face the sun
his gaze unafraid,
emboldened.[17]

Inspired, she dictates her first letter.

I, as worthless,
and even more than worthless
with the name of woman,
and despite all my fears and uncertainties,
I am sure my visions are good and Divine,
for like the light of the sun
my heart is entirely inflamed,
and I want to be allowed
to enkindle other hearts.[18]

Bernard of Clairvaux,
theologian and scholar,
receives her letter
reads her writings,
hears her humble need for validation,
gives her writing to the new Pope, Eugenius.

She, the lowliest of the lowly, a woman,
taught by an unlearned woman[19]
confesses her visions.

This letter to Bernard,
is her weapon against Abbot Kuno.
Her secret is revealed.
Now she would rather die
than suppress it.

Silence, would be my gravest sin now.
she tells Volmar
even if it means
an inquisition,
even death.

Facing a Papal Envoy

The sun commences its return.
Hildegard dreads the sound of cracking ice
for her protective, winter cocoon will pass.
Rumour of a papal envoy
is what she fears
and what she wishes with all her being.

She warns her band of sisters.
Kuno is as glacial as the winter days.

Just days before the Lenten fast begins
distant horns, then thunder of hooves
rise above the chanted prayers of sext.

The sisters fall silent,
kneel in fear.
Richardis embraces Hildegard
as they listen
to commotion of horses and men.

Abbot Kuno calls for the Magistra.
All eighteen sisters appear
in front of their small Kapelle,
braced behind Hildegard,
bewildered, afraid they might lose her
this very day.

Abbot Kunos's eyes bulge.
A papal envoy,
an inquisition sent by the Pope,
Bishops Alberto and Adalbert
await you in the chapter room,
shouts Abbot Kuno.
They will not have my tolerance!

The cobbled courtyard,
reeks of manure and sweat.
In red robes some with purple cowls
men with avarice in their eyes,
servants in striped gold and blue
busy themselves with horses
and self-important chatter.
Refreshments divert them
and they appear less overbearing.

Head high, Hildegard steps forward.
Her eyes do not betray the thoughts
of her racing mind.
Can my writings be burnt
like that of Abelard in France?
Could I be forbidden to write again?
What if I am accused of heresy?
What of excommunication.?

Divine Revelation

The chapter room is cold.
Hildegard is not deterred.
Fear is dimmed.
Like stars in a dark sky
her eyes beam light.
She stands before them, not the weak female
that she confesses to be
but as a prophet of her day.

The bishops sit high on large carved chairs.
Abbot Kuno sits with a severe frown
behind an oak desk against the wall.
His impatient tap of fingers
does not deter Hildegard. Her voice
comes from a deep inner knowing
her words stun the bishops.

The Divine Light calls me
like the light of the sun,
it entirely inflames my heart
to enkindle other hearts
so that imagination and creativity,
forgiveness and contrition
might flow again in the world.[20]

With the Trinitarian question
she speaks the truth of her vision:
Christ in bright light,
radiating out, glowing fire
that illuminates all of creation,
so that the three are one light in one power.[21]
She bedazzles her interrogators.

The papal envoy leaves enlivened,
carries positive stories of a holy lady.

Days pass in a cone of silence.
A missive arrives from the monk Bernard,
Your visions, were read by Pope Eugenius
at the Synod of Triers.
The papal envoy calls your words inspired.
You are requested to continue,
continue to write what you see and hear.[22]

Out the scriptorium window
the sky is hand-painted gold.
For Hildegard fire and water, air and earth
shine in wonder and oneness.
The almond trees burst into bloom.
Leaves shimmer with light.
Frolicking water of the rocky Nahr
slips joyfully along towards the distant Rhine.

Rule of Authority

Word of Hildegard spreads.
From Mainz to Koblenz and Cologne.
Even her local bishop, Henry,
proudly proclaims her.

More pilgrims arrive,
Hildegard, the pinpoint of light
bursts forth
grows brighter.

As more hear of her healing ways
infirmary days are even busier.

The convent grows.
Sisters and postulants
pray, sing and study,
work in the garden and infirmary.
A new sister, Clara,
daughter of a noble family north of Bavaria,
brings knowledge of Latin, a boon
for study of plants and healing.

Abbot Kuno is inflamed
by prospect of glory,
abundant pilgrim gifts,
rich dowries from his sisters.
He plots to manipulate a rich
easy future for his monastery –
with new buildings
new dormitory for the sisters
a hostel for travellers
extra garden space.
Yet, in him
rages a cauldron
of jealousy and anger.
At every turn he finds a way
for his authority to rule.
Demands obedience.

Volmar is a tense observer.
When he comments he is silenced.
The rule requires obedience.

Divine Command

Hildegard stands before Abbot Kuno,
stares at him and his priors
as if gazing into a void.

Her voice defiant,
Until this day
we have found our contentment.
Now we are twenty sisters
and three new requests.
I, as magistra, ask your blessing.
In all humility as a fragile human,
my vision instructs us to be wayfarers
to St Rupert's hill by the Rhine.
An abandoned hermitage
we can establish a space for us to grow.

It is a Divine command.

If Kuno's shocked eyes could diminish her
she would be diminished.
She clasps her hands
reassures herself of her own presence.

He rises, turns away
swings back to face her,
his voice frigid,
You have no permission.
The sisters are vowed here at Disibodenberg.
Your new convent is here.
The monastery relies on your revenue,
the pilgrims that come,
the infirmary, gardens, even your name,
your writings that I have allowed.

You have no blessing.
He stabs his index finger
to dismiss her.

Hildegard remains
resolute,
even as his words dagger her heart
her answer is quiet, calm,

Here we are. It is early spring,
there is growth all around,
the grass shoots,
apple trees burst to fullness,
barn swallows nest,
larks play on riffling wing.

Here I am,
there is a tremble on her lips,
living here thirty-six winters.
A tree dried and barren
a tree never yet come to leaf.
Growth stunted…

She falls silent,
her mouth dry,
holds back an avalanche of pain.
She gazes into the distance,
straightens up
looks directly at him.

It is in your petulance
you deny us blessing.

She turns her back
walks out.

Ending

Abbot Kuno remains truculent,
absolute power cripples him.
At mealtimes he assumes full stature,
preaches obedience to his monks.

White-knuckled, he grips the podium
reads from the *The Rule of St Benedict*,
As soon as anything is ordered by the superior
let there be no delay in obedience.
…remember the sloth of disobedience.[23]
Monks listen and nod intently,
he closes the book hard.
Each time Volmar listens
his heart feels torn.

Beyond authority,
beyond rage,
beyond this demand of holy obedience,
Hildegard collapses.
Her book of Divine visions
falls silent
unfinished.

In a damp obscure cell
heavy with darkness,
Hildegard refuses food, her face pales
hollow-cheeked and eyes glazed.
She feels Richardis's tender hands
her smooth and gentle touch. Her sisters
surround her straw-filled pallet
as around a dying bed,
fear her last words.
Three weeks she lies.

Life or Death

Distraught, Volmar intervenes.
He writes directly
to Bishop Henry in Mainz,
Holy Hildegard, the seer
who writes her visions, is dying.
We will not have the completion of her manuscript.

Bishop Henry dispatches a missive,
calls for her release.
Abbot Kuno receives it, flings it down,
stamps on its seal –
Her life or death is of no concern.
She belongs here, we love her.
For 36 years she has been ours.
Now, even her death will draw pilgrims.

Bishop Henry finally sends a decree
to override the abbot.
His emissary arrives on horseback.

Richardis whispers to Hildegard
Be strong my sister,
our bishop wants you to continue to write,
demands the abbot free you and us all.

In this winter of her days,
Hildegard stirs, smiles,
encouraged with warm fennel broth,
and precious colostrum soaked spelt.

She softly speaks,
my visions are still with me.

Summoned

Abbot Kuno summons Hildegard.

With her little returning strength,
pale, frail,
she leans on her sister Richardis,
faces the abbot.

His face puce with rage
he shouts
You go.
His hand jolts,
points to the door.

This writing you have not finished,
I do not want the fire of hell on me,
I do not want this monastery to be under an edict.
Pope Eugenius has commanded.
Now I command.
You go.
You go to this old hermitage near Bingen
without my blessing.

He comes around in front of the table
looms over her, his rage triumphant,
but without Volmar, without your dowries
always as prioress under me.

Garnering Support

Hildegard feels a surge of hope,
a spur to action.
Membrane of change thins.
She walks to the scriptorium
already abuzz with tactical commotion.
Her mind stirs to rally her allies.

Volmar scribes her words.
She dictates missives to Bernard
and his monks for support,
to the burgers of Bingen for help,
to inform the Bishop of Mainz.
Richardis, alert to Hildegard's every need
calls for patronage from her mother,
Marchioness von Stade.

Outside the window
there is also tactical commotion.
Open-mouthed fledglings,
satisfied only for an instant,
when their parents fill their mouths,
flutter and fluster.
The barn swallows circle
encouraging their young
to fly and feed themselves.
Spring bursts in the linden trees.

Bernard answers her call.
Makeshift accommodation will be readied,
his monks will build for her.
Lady von Stade's patronage avowed.
Bingen is ready.

Hildegard looks beyond to the hills,
sees their seasonal beauty,
their formidable deeply rooted presence,
Give me faith for my sisters.
She draws herself up. Stands straight,
hears her way guided with a whispering voice,

O mountain on high
you will never weaken in God's test,
but you stand far off like an exile.
The armoured man does not have power
to seize you.
You are glorious in your preparation for God.[24]

Leaves quiver in the light.
Is it a wink?
A smile?
Her world opens,
a cracking chrysalis.
Her sisters rally to her blessing,
O daughter of the Way,
as the seed planted deeply
dies to itself,
so too do you die.
Now it is in dying to self
you live.

You live.

V
1150–1152

Give me wings of determination and kindness, so I can soar above the stars of heaven, using Your good will. You and Your holiness are all I need. Make me Your zither of love.
– Hildegard of Bingen, *Book of Life's Merits*

Leaving Disibodenberg

Pre-dawn prayer complete,
twenty-three sisters gather
breathe crisp spring air.
In flicker of oil lanterns
shadows mingle on cloister walls.

Hildegard strides out
holds a lantern high,
her face partly illuminated
by its swaying pale light.
Creases at her eyes and mouth
aver to her fifty-two years.
Richardis catches her determined stance,
shoulders confident in their burden.

Palfreys stamp and whinny
girths are tightened
mail rattles, the soldier-escort ready
peasants huddle, chatter
amongst commotion, buzz of tension.
A cock crow pierces the air.

Out of the darkness
a figure leads a smoky-grey horse.

Volmar!
Hildegard gasps.
He nods assurance, whispers,
I could not let you go alone.
Relief, sighs around the cloister.

Abbot Kuno and the priors,
arms folded, stunned into silence.
A scowl of stone statues.

*We will sing our journey
away from these shadowed walls.*
Hildegard calls,
Let faith be our compass.

Dawn peers through a light mist.
With song, rumble of carts, hoof beats
Hildegard and her sisters depart.

Creating Rupertsberg

How their voices soar.
O viridissima virgo ave…[25]
An exodus to a promised land,
fifteen miles along the Nahr
at its junction with the Rhine.

They cross the stone bridge
along the Roman Way.

Volmar rides ahead to prepare for them.
Peasants from nearby greet them,
take their horses and provide refreshments.

Hildegard and her sisters climb to the top of a knoll.
Exhausted, exhilarated, they stand arm in arm,
near the crumbling ruins
of St Rupert's 8th century hermitage.
The Rhine River ribbons below
like wings of freedom.

Hildegard raises her eyes to heaven
sweeps her arms upwards in gratitude,
breathes deeply.
Let us give thanks,
our new home will rise here.

She pictures the buildings,
here at the confluence of rivers.
Our abbey will be the heart of Bingen
part of its trade, commerce,
its estates, community and vineyards.

She piles up a few stones,
We will restore this hermitage.
She sways, almost falls.
Richardis rushes
to support her weary friend.

We will have comfortable dormitories.
Just imagine, plumbing, ablutions,
baths and piped water.
The sisters chatter, clap excitedly.

Hildegard points down the hill,
Let us plant our gardens near that old orchard.
Working together, they will thrive.
Visualise an apotheka, a scriptorium.
But first an infirmary,
our own infirmary.

Hildegard looks over at Clara
with her fresh rosy cheeks.
Clara unable to hide her joy
looks taller,
smiles eagerly, claps again.

The local people, especially
the women of Bingen town
will work with us.

As Hildegard looks around
she sees three of her sisters
standing apart,
talking among themselves.

Dissent Emboldens Hildegard

The three sisters still wrapped
in black travelling capes,
stand beside the temporary sleeping quarters,
their hunched figures a picture of misery.
Hildegard approaches,
they drop their eyes.
Guda, Adeline, Wilfredis, what is it?

We…didn't expect this, Guda sulks,
it is too makeshift.
We want to return…to what we know.
Wilfredis, an older widow whimpers,
this is too hard,
hides her face.

Shocked, Hildegard takes a sharp breath,
My sisters, enough grumbling.
We are all weary.
Hildegard struggles
to keep the quiver from her voice.

Guda, I know you well.
I need your support to set up our kitchen garden.
You will supervise the peasants from Bingen,
they want to work with us.
We will seek plants from the four winds,
acquire manuscripts, create healing medicines
to make us all proud. You will be proud.

Hildegard chides louder, her voice assertive,
Adeline, you are well skilled
in selection of leaves for healing teas.
Wilfredis you are so keen
to concoct our salves.
This is our new beginning.
We will build, with the local people.

Guda's shoulders shift under her coarse tunic.
Adeline keeping her eyes downcast,
edges nearer to Hildegard.

Hildegard points at wild grape vines tangled
and twirling over neglected apple trees.
See, the old orchard
will give us work immediately.
Come my sisters, dulce viriditas.
Volmar awaits,
let us join the others in the tent for vespers.

Twenty-three voices
sing on holy ground.
The Nahr runs down from the mountains
plays into the Rhine below,
that pulses a sturdy busy lifeline
to a world outside itself.
Threads of smoke
sigh in the breeze
from the village of Bingen.

Sense of Purpose

Hildegard muses
how wise it was
to lug the carts
bringing dried herbs and plants,
even rose cuttings from the garden.

Even before the infirmary is set up,
a mother arrives with her son
from a hamlet outside Bingen,
the child poorly, his eyes oozing.

Hildegard, holy lady, have pity, she pleads.

Hildegard blesses them both.
Clara prepares a compress
from pounded field mint,
grown, picked and dried in Disibodenberg,
ties it into a cloth binding his eyes.
Each day his mother brings him
until he sees and smiles again.

News of Hildegard reaches
up and down the Rhine.
Pilgrims line up.
Hildegard listens, counsels, blesses,
rests her healing hands on them.
Some stay at the makeshift infirmary.

Hildegard uses knowledge
gleaned from Volmar's books,
assists Clara and the sisters
to prepare
local leaves, flowers and berries
for healing teas, salves and tinctures.

Guda and her workers
prepare the gardens,
hyssop, fennel, parsley, borage, sage.
Her sisters search out native plants
encouraged by local peasants.
Hildegard observes and intuits much.
Soon, she muses,
we will have our own writings about healing.

A New Earth

Among the fleur-de-lis
spilling across the hillside
above the Rhine,
gardens bloom, buildings rise,
a Benedictine abbey evolves.
Its pillars – prayer, work, study.

Today, Hildegard makes her way
to the rudimentary scriptorium.
Pauses with artisans and local labourers.
She watches the master mason fashion
intricate carvings for the chapel's entrance,
runs her hand across the rough hewn stone
hauled up from the river,
admires the first of many arches.

Her sisters bid her welcome
to their crowded infirmary,
the sick brighten at her blessing.
Her new Sister Inez looks up
with merry dark eyes.
Hildegard notices
her fine-boned aristocratic face
as she tucks strands of black hair
behind her veil.
Inez, a self-taught scholar
teaches her sisters Latin,
at Hildegard's request.

She checks the climbing roses
planted against the old hermitage wall,
nods her head with satisfaction.
They have survived winter struggle,
a memory from where they came,
…to make the invisible visible,
Richardis had whispered playfully
when they had planted them together.

Sister Clara with her warm cheerfulness
is absorbed in the fledgling apotheke.
Local plants and herbs
add to the knowledge and treatments
brought from Disibodenberg.

Hildegard looks across the gardens
pleased to see Guda with her workers,
breathes in the scented blooms of jasmine.
Raspberry leaves catch her attention,
crunches them between her fingers,
murmurs approval,
almost ready for the teas.

Hildegard's cherished time,
is in the makeshift scriptorium.
Volmar and Richardis work
on her book, nearly complete.
Their silence broken only by the scratch of quill,
tinkle of ink bottles, shuffle of palette.
Breathing excitedly,
Hildegard sits near the window,
closes her eyes
whispers the beginning of her new vision,

only the clang of the prayer bell
breaks her reverie.

Cosmic Web

A year passes
in rhythmic ding
of carpenters and masons.
The new abbey rises
with artistry and skill.
Word spreads along the Rhine.
Artisans travel from Chartres
bring new knowledge.
Storytellers share news,
scholars debate ideas.

Through this window on the world
Volmar hears of valuable manuscripts,
sends for them, to copy for their abbey.
Hildegard and Richardis devour
these writings.

Hildegard's world expands.
Our earth, the visible universe
is a unified whole.
Light glows within and around her
She creates a mandala, the universe,
in the feminine shape of an egg,
all connected in its cosmic web of creation.

With nature's help
humankind can set into creation
all that is life sustaining.[26]
She ponders.

Unearthing Heaven

Seamless fold of seasons.
Not so seamless, daily struggle.
Life is still comfortless,
harsh, rough.

Music carries them.
Singing gladdens them.

Hildegard is invigorated
by harmonies of sound,
sees music in the dawn,
light on the hills,
in the caress of the wind,
shape of the clouds,
sound of the entwining rivers,
the patter of rain,
chatter of verdant tendrils of vine.

Music moves in her mind
fills her writing
defines her day.
She sings with her sisters.
Her sisters sing with her.

Singing softens their tired
discouraged hearts
like blossoms soften stone walls.

In giving voice to her poetry
Hildegard bursts into song.
Words of Divine Light,
sounds from the heavenly spheres
echo in her,
O fleeting soul, be strong.
Clothe yourself in the armour of light.
You are surrounded
with the embrace of Divine mysteries.[27]

She sees creation, a symphony
of joy and jubilation,
a great chorus
of the cosmos itself.

In the garden with her sisters
she draws lines with a stick on the earth
dots out the shift of sounds,
with the stick as baton and pointer
she teaches them her new music.
Their eyes shine.
Her antiphons and canticles
enrich the Divine Office.
Richardis leads, her voice ethereal,
the sisters join, words and rhythms soar,
breathless notes, higher and ever higher.[28]

Their unfinished church
embraces their song,
a new heaven and new earth.

First Opera

In a vision
Hildegard has her sisters
sing as personified virtues
in song and action.
She sees struggle
against the devil,
visualises it played out as drama.
Volmar can take the part of the devil.
He will not sing. She ponders aloud.

All abuzz, she hastens to tell Richardis.
With Volmar as scribe
they create their first opera.
Hildegard writes the words and notes,
Richardis plucks the psaltery
sings softly,
her radiance caught in a stream of light

Their eyes catch,
mirror harmony of purpose.

Hildegard's thoughts drift back
to the eight-year-old Richardis,
who looked to her as mother,
and the one
whose tender hands held her,
cared for her, in her sickness.
Now at twenty-two a grown woman.

The Art of Perseverance

It is 1151, late winter.
Ten years have passed
since Hildegard dictated her first vision
in the old Disibodenberg monastery.
Now these inspired words
are ready for the world.
Two hundred and thirty parchments,
a hundred and fifty thousand words
with thirty-four illuminations.
Music, poetry and her first opera,
stacked, in the carrel
waiting for a title and to be bound.

Volmar smiles,
remembers the single quire of parchment
he once prepared.
He affirms her,
you awaken us to the holiness of the earth
in cosmic justice and healing.
Many will be consoled by your words.
May they never fall into forgetfulness
but be heard in the midst of love.
Hildegard beams at Volmar.
She looks out at the gently curving hills
reflects on ten years of struggle,
the journey to here,
a sacred text in love and trust
and the art of perseverance.

Her years are divided by liturgical feasts
her days marked by the hours
time, by the moon and seasons
rhythmic flow of the cycles.
Abbot Kuno's stubborn
withhold of dowries constrains her.
Yet nothing constrains her spirit.

Oh, how her spirit soars.
The opera must be performed
for our new chapel opening,

Discernment

Alone in the orchard after Lenten vespers,
the title for her book stirs and quickens.
Underfoot the crack of frosted ground
tingles, dances through her.
Her mind jolts back in time
to when she stood before Abbot Kuno
in sandals and knitted socks
on the eve of Jutta's funeral,
when nothing could prevent
the bite of frost chill her.

Bare trees scratch the throat of evening,
ignite her tongue, inspiration flames,
she exclaims a new thought,
sings a new word,
Scito vias Domini,
Scivias, she sings,
Know the Way of the Lord.

With steps light as a breeze
she wings her way back,
seeks out Volmar and Richardis.

Scivias
will be the tile of my book,
she declares.
They huddle, a holy triumvirate
in the dim candlelit scriptorium.
Volmar scribes the word *Scivias*
decorates with gold leaf.
Richardis with the most precious of the inks
illumines the covering parchment.

Anticipation

1

The chill and fallow of white fields
gives way to vegetable gardens for pottage stew.
The sisters prune, pickle and preserve,
plait the garlic
to hang from the cross-pull beams,
prepare dried seeds for spring,
gather leaves for medicinal teas,
take turns to press the grapes.
They sing and plan for their opera,
rise above drudgery of daily living.

2

Vernal freshness brings inspiration.
On the branch beyond her window
buds wait to blossom.
Hildegard's mind bustles with ideas,
busy as the Rhine below where
ships and cargo barges
ply their way.
The excitement of the coming opera
waits to unfold.

Touch of Silk

There must have been a moment
when the idea arose.
Maybe it was the visions
when holy virtues spoke to her.

Maybe when all fifty sisters spent time
laughing together as they picked grapes
for the wine press,
to make the sacramental altar wine
and their sweet wine
to give warmth and strengthen blood,
as Hildegard says.

Maybe it was the day
the cousins Bertrude and Agnes
from a noble family joined her sisters,
proudly announcing they were seamstresses
and donating reams of silk
for priestly albs and vestments.

Just maybe, the touch of the silk
gave Hildegard the idea.

Excitement drives her thoughts and words
as she muses and then reflects out loud,
My sisters will wear silk gowns
as they sing our opera.
We will have it ready to perform
for the bishop and his entourage
at the consecration of our new chapel.

After matins,
Hildegard gathers her sisters,
My sisters, God loves beauty.
For our opera we will dress
as noble regal souls.
We will wear silk gowns that flow.
Gold wreaths and flower circlets will crown us.
Let our hair loose under light translucent veils.
Our hair is our glory,
not a temptation to cut or hide.

Feverish as excited children
the sisters sew and sing
and with every practice
Hildegard watches their confidence grow.

All Invited

Amid the blossoms of their second Easter
birds fly to and fro building nests
and Hildegard sends out her invitations.
Music will bring light to the dark.
Stillness will become dancing.
The Bishop of Mainz
will bless our newly built church.
There is to be a concert.
All are welcome.

Word travels around Bingen,
murmurs brush the courts of Mainz.
Peasant families
walk from local hamlets and towns.
The Lords and Bishop are edgy yet curious.
Priests assemble from all over the Rhineland
intrigued but wary of the *Holy Lady*
and her visions.

Showcasing the Abbey

An early spring afternoon
illumines vividness of robes and gowns.
Hospitality of the new abbey
welcomes lively entourages,
bishops, priests, monks, dignitaries, clerics.
The Marchioness von Stade,
a rare visit to her daughter at Rupertsberg,
and the largest audience
ever seen in Bingen arrive.
After the bishop's blessing of the church
Hildegard and her sisters,
walk, poised and noble
in splendid procession
down the aisle in long flowing gowns of silk
singing glorious, heavenly music.
They circle the altar
dazzling brides of Christ
singing their opera, a morality play,[29]
virtues triumphant, vices subdued,
the struggle of the human soul
with the wiles of the devil.

Hildegard catches
the marchioness's shocked gaze
focused on her confident beautiful daughter.
When the sisters harmonise in a chorus
and Richardis sings the solo to end the opera
tears fill Hildegard's eyes,
she bows her head.

After vespers that evening
the last meal before lenten fast
their excitement and pride is palpable.

Admonishment rains down like the Rhine
after a snow melt.
This domineering woman holds my daughter back,
Marchioness von Stade stabs at Volmar.
Her sisters too free, says another angrily.
Her sisters too visible, says another.

Outside her window the oak resists the wildest storms.
Hildegard stands defiant, against all criticism.

VI
1152–1157

Disruption

A request interrupts Rupertsberg,
The Marchioness von Stade calls for her daughter
Richardis, to become abbess of an abbey in Bassum.

Hildegard rushes a missive through Volmar
declines the request,
I beg you – don't upset my soul so much
that you make me cry angry tears.
I beg you. Don't cut me to the quick.
Don't wound me deeply
over my most beloved daughter, Richardis.
Even now I see her in my mind,
wearing pearls made of virtues
radiant as the dawn-blush.
This snatching of her from us
is absolutely, absolutely, absolutely not God's will.[30]

The response shifts to a demand,
Hartwig the archbishop
has acquired for his sister, Richardis,
a position of influence as abbess.

Hildegard retorts fiercely,
You do not know what you are doing
when you scatter the work founded by God,
in favour of opportunities to make money.
In favour of the human wickedness of men,
who do not heed the fear of the Lord.[31]

Finally an ultimatum,
Henry, Archbishop of Mainz,
decrees an escort will convey
Richardis to her new abbey in Bassum.

Hildegard's skin prickles,
her body tightens.
She gazes into the distance and dictates,
Beware of the buying and selling of offices, remember
the fate of Nebuchadnezzar another all powerful man
whom the Light cast from his throne
for his pride and rash decisions.[32]

Paralysis

The eve of the Passover has come,
Richardis, ordered to her new abbey by Easter.

Before the Passover Mass is ended
her entourage arrives at the gate.
From the church they hear
commotion, flurry of activity,
snort of restless horses
as they are watered and fed.
Couriers, escorts and soldiers
fiddle impatiently.

From the altar, Volmar, eyes downcast,
calls Richardis forward.
With faltering steps, she walks to the altar,
sways slightly as if her body catches a breeze.
Burnt down wax candles flicker
on her pale alabaster skin.
A blue vein ticks on her neck.
Volmar blesses her, *Go in peace.*

Hildegard's feet feel stuck.
Volmar looks down to her,
she approaches the altar,
lays her trembling hands
on Richardis's shoulders,
kisses her on each cheek.
Hildegard reaches up
to brush away a tear,
their hands touch.

Hildegard gazes upon her for the last time
looks away, walks back to her pew.

She remembers telling Richardis
when she was a young girl,
how singing helps through hard times.

Caught in a choke of tears
the processional song is loud and fervent.

As they emerge from their newly built church
a loud call of some strange bird
wails in the distance.
With a clatter of fading hooves
Richardis is gone.

Betrayed

Hildegard shivers in gelid air.
Her empty arms ache,
her loss too deep for words.
Torn between disbelief and fury,
pain's deep wound.

Her breath is dry, sharp,
her body wrenched with sorrow.
She is drained,
like sun-scorched grass
bent, bowed, burdened
with not only loss but betrayal.

After Vespers,
in the solace of darkness
Hildegard sits head in hands,
the absence of Richardis unbearable.
Her mind spins into giddiness,
trying to grasp the sense of her loss,
their mutual bond of stability,
their abhorrence of simony
their plans and dreams
to fulfil the will of the Divine.

Her hand shakes
as she writes on her tablet
for Volmar to scribe,

I love you for your noble bearing,
your wisdom, your purity, your soul and all your life.
Now I have this to say: alas for me, a mother
and alas for me, a daughter.
I am forsaken as an orphan
Let all mourn with me,
who have ever had such high love in heart and mind
for a human being as I for you.[33]

Grief Comes Hard

For Hildegard
light struggles with darkness.
Her emptiness rages like the surging waters
at the confluence of the rivers below.

She stares around her dim cell,
glances at abandoned tablets and parchments
piled on her writing table –
meaningless without Richardis.

Plans for the guest house,
new manuscripts on the Cosmos,
writings on her medical insights,
new discoveries on healing plants,
the treatise on Saints Ursula and Rupert
and still Saint Disibod to be finished.
She picks up a few listlessly,
notes the headings and drops them.

She endures compline,
takes her escape
into the privacy of her cell
kneels at her prie-dieu
stares out her window.

The sky still holds its light
when all she waits for these past days
is the comfort of the brooding dark of night.
Even the clouds grieve.

Resilience

At Pentecost
Hildegard sings the music
she composed for Richardis.
Benedictine rhythm, small comfort
to her heavy heart.

Incessant demands frustrate.
Hildegard's head aches.
Another knock. *Will they ever stop?*
This time it is Sister Clara
seeking urgent help.

Hildegard follows her,
to the infirmary.
She blinks in surprise
at the crowds spilling out into the courtyard.
A pang of guilt clouds her mind
for the new building plans sit on her desk.

Activity shocks her from the trance of grief.
Three of her postulants, with local help
prepare herbs from the garden.
In a corner she sees Sister Inez
confidently instruct
a mother on the use of lungwort tincture.
Many bow, reach out for blessing,
touch her tunic as she passes.

Clara leads her to a curtained corner,
Hildegard smells the fear,
hears the muffled moans,
before she sees the young woman curled
into the straw pallet
exhausted from days of labor.
Clara crouches, takes her trembling hand,
reassures her,
Sister Hildegard is here.

They give her sips of fennel steeped in mulled wine,
rub in the red carnelian quartz stone,
whisper the invocation to Saint Margaret
over and over into ceaseless litany.
The girl's eyes, terrified, plead with Hildegard.

Pain sweeps them along.
Hildegard calls for Inez
to set up an inhalation, ground seed and balsam,
calls for pig fat, flaxseed oil.
Inez applies poultices of wild ginger and fennel.
Clara brings the stone of jasper
for the girl to clasp
and sits rubbing her hand.
The litany blends into breathing,
into the breath of life and death
as pain ebbs and flows.

An oil lantern wick flickers.
Hildegard's deft hands move,
massage, manipulate.
Her fingers find a tiny foot, another,
a baby struggles into the world
gulps a first breath, life's first cry.
She looks to their care,
watches the baby girl find her mother's breast.
Inez brings warm bone broth and honeyed jelly.

Hildegard finds her smile,
nods to Clara and Inez,
becomes aware of her own deep breathing
filling the hollowness of her grief.

Later in the orchard,
a place where only blackbirds call
she plays her hand along the ivy-wild wall,
confesses to Volmar,
An incident today in the infirmary
has brought me back.
I am reminded of my glad embrace of life
There is so much to do.

Renewed Fervour

Matins is over.
As the sun's sturdy rays hit the hills
Hildegard strides out. Her resolute gait
bespeaks a new determination.
She seeks out the artisans and builders
and spreads out her scrolls before them.

They survey her plans
a real infirmary and hostel of welcome
Excited nods
buzz of conversation.

Her steps become buoyant
as she approaches the Scriptorium,
with its familiar smells of vellum
and beeswax worked into bindings.
She finds Volmar, seated on a stool
at the end of his carrel,
quill in hand.
He copies Chartres' *Cosmographia*.

Hildegard sits,
gazes at each parchment in turn
with unflinching attention,
absorbing the text.

She looks up.
Volmar notices her eyes
deepen with intensity.
She presents her new writings,
scratched words on her wax tablets
and scribbled compilations.

She sits higher on the stool
her back tall,
I feel this new clarity,
like morning after thick fog.
I am called to write again.
she says in a hesitant voice,
I am ready…with your help,
to begin a new book.
It is revealed to me,
how creation is filled
with mysterious healing forces.

Volmar smiles his encouragement.
Hildegard's face folds into a frown.
She crumbles, chokes back words,
…need Ricardis,
she fills her lungs with a deep sigh,
mumbles with an awkward smile,
…her roses grow well on the garden wall,
it would make her so happy.

Hildegard brushes her cheek.
Volmar eases over,
places his hand on hers,
Hush my sister, do not speak. I beg you.
Clara is well schooled in Latin.
She can join us here.
Wilfredis is trained now for the infirmary,
…will take over.

Hildegard taps her fingers on the cumdach,
and speaks with renewed enthusiasm,
I see and hear the Cosmos.
in all its healing powers for humanity.
In tree and plant and animal,
and gemstones in all their colours
is given the composition of medicine.[34]

It is 1153.

Volmar sees her impatience to begin.
Reassures her,
I am your scribe. Is that not enough?
She laughs. *It is enough.*

Sister Clara

'Creation looks upon its creator
like the beloved upon her lover'[35]

Before Hildegard enters the garden
it announces itself
with crush of lemon balm and wild mint.
She hears hum of Odelia's bees
grateful for the honey she bottles,
and of course the wax for the book binding.
Hildegard notes how Guda's garden thrives,
sees pride beam from her village workers.
The hawthorn hedge
with its burst of red blossom
runs along the north side of the wall.

She smells aroma of fermenting grapes
and herbal brews
as she enters the area
that Clara calls St Rupert's Apotheka.
Hildegard finds Clara and Wilfredis
working at a timber bench,
mortar and pestle in hand.
Wilfredis shows her the white elderflowers
found growing wild on the edge of the tree line.

Hildegard looks intently at both of them,
suggests Volmar's idea of change.
Clara and Wilfredis embrace in joy.
Honoured and excited
Clara reaches out, wraps Hildegard
in her soft arms,
and Wilfredis's keen eyes shine.
They notice a smile
crease Hildegard's face.

Fiery Light of Writing

Bright blue days
light the high south windows
of the scriptorium with its vegetable
oaky smell of newly ground gall-nuts.

Hildegard opens her arms
wide as if to seize
this new beginning.

Sister Clara sits at a carrel
haloed in the light
flushed with happiness.
Some parchments finished
her pen-work flourishes
down the margins.

Volmar's tall figure,
shoulders slightly stooped now
enters and nods his greeting,
comments on the window's good light,
takes newly prepared quills from the carrel.
Red and blue inks
usually kept for finest works
are already unlidded.
Hildegard claps excitedly.

Scivias, cover illumined
in gold-leafed splendour
looks down from the highest shelf.
A talisman.

Gatherings of blank parchment
wait full of possibility.
Clara reaches for a new sheet.
Volmar watches eagerly.

A cosmic web of creation
wings into Hildegard's mind
her hand covers her heart
to cradle its ache for expression.
She breathes into the light.
All one,
sing the leaves of the trees outside
a choir of hosannas tremble along branches
their tracery gilded, fiery gold against the sky.

All one
whirs each drop of water in the Nahr
as it gurgles along
to become one with the Rhine.

Eyes to the heavens,
Hildegard looks into the heart of light,
dictates to Volmar and Clara.

I have exalted humans with the vocation of creation,
into a oneness with all creation.
Humankind is called to co-create.
All nature is a vital inclusion.
Without it we cannot survive.[36]

At times she steeples her fingers in thought
voice hardly audible,
at times she dictates from her wax tablets.
Empty parchments fill
like stars stipple across a night sky.

Eyes wide open she invokes,
The oneness of creation and humanity
demands justice.
We know fields will no longer yield their fruits
where human greed and injustice
have sought too quick a yield.[37]

From the fertile fields of her mind
Hildegard crafts words
to comfort, console, confront and castigate.
Under the stamp of papal approval
embedded in an era of superstition
her words have power.
Her strange pure tongue
captivates bishops and kings,
filters through all social classes.

Her presence, her writings, her preaching
offer the hope of change,
a chance to make sense of the world.

Death of Richardis

After none
Hildegard lingers in the chapel,
to plan with artisans from Chartres,
murals of Saint Ursula's story
on the walls of the church.

Volmar comes in,
face grim, tight.
My dear Sister,
there is word…from Bassum.

Hildegard turns sharply.
He beckons her to join him in the orchard.

They stand in the shadow of the hawthorn hedge.
How it has grown, she murmurs.
She looks over at the row of linden trees
nearly ready for their first harvest,
her face flushes
remembering the delight
she and Richardis and Clara had
the day they worked with the gardeners
to plant them.

Volmar covers his arms
in the folds of his robe,
my dear one
it is Richardis.
Hildegard frowns uneasily,
has she agreed to return?
I have heard, she is not happy.

*My dear one I bring sad news,
Richardis had fever... has passed,
It was last month. She died.*

Hildegard steadies herself
on a hawthorn branch.
A thorn pierces her skin, draws blood.
Hildegard groans, the hills echo
then silence.

Hildegard does not know childbirth
but she doubles over
as if something was being ripped out
from inside her.

Volmar extends his arm to comfort.
She leans against the orchard wall
pale and breathless.

They watch the mountains
on the other side of the Rhine
shawled in afternoon rays of light.

Hildegard's jawline,
shadows a twitch in her neck
as she absorbs the detail
and ponders finality of loss.

I wonder if she asked for me[38]
Hildegard whispers.

The wolf of betrayal burns her throat,
rages in her mind,
how Richardis's family
plundered her sister with impunity.

White violets nearby
nod in the afternoon breeze
which suddenly chills
whipped up from the river below.

On the way back
her step falters.
The tumble of Richardis's rose
falls with grace across its wall.

Correspondence

Within the utter swoon of grief
only the frame of music
and praying the hours holds her.
Unable to dwell on memories
Hildegard measures her days
with their new demands.
Her reputation ripples around Europe.
Popes, bishops, even kings
seek her advice.
Volmar scribes her replies
in Latin, sometimes Germanic tongue.
Invitations to visit
come from abbeys and monasteries.
Her eyes widen
at the thought of such journeys.

Hildegard may have words of comfort
and consolation for local peasants
but for those in authority,
seeking affirmation and surety of salvation
from the *holy lady*, the seer,
her barb-sharp letters
warn and challenge.
There is no assuaging
greed or hypocrisy.
As for Abbot Kuno demanding Volmar back
she calls him a thief.

In correspondence with King Henry,
Hildegard consoles but reminds him
of his responsibility as leader.
She calls him to discern,
Beware the dark bird flying
in from the evil north squawking
'you're powerful'.[39]

Eleanor

Queen Eleanor was to poets
what dawn is to birds.
Salutations sung by minstrels
were to a queen of beauty.
Troubadours and balladeers
sang her story along the pilgrim routes.

Educated at court,
Eleanor garners her wisdom
from a motley assembly
of vassals, castellans,
princes and feudal lords.
She absorbs it all.

Two women reach out.
Hildegard and Eleanor
conduct a dance of correspondence.

To answer Queen Eleanor
Hildegard takes time
awaits the Divine Light,
and dictates to Volmar.

My dear Queen,
you are an inspiration to many.
You know a courtly world of which I am not familiar.
You know the land, vineyards and olive groves
and sheepfolds rood by rood.
You know the vast agglomeration of hamlets and towns.
The storm pounding your brain is your panic.
It makes you unable to rest.
Steady yourself by relying on God.
He'll help you now, when you need him,
and so will those around you.
Be calm.
My blessing is with you.[40]

Seer of Destiny

Frederick Barbarossa is crowned
King, Holy Roman Emperor.
The world waits in terror.
He plunders villages
sacks monasteries
monks and nuns flee.
The Bishop of Mainz takes flight.
Fire on the horizon, smoke
the colour of tears.
Barbarossa's message;
Woe to those who spurn me.
By my own power, I do away
with their obstinacy and rebellion.

Hildegard turns to Volmar.
The Divine Light calls me to speak out,
to dare say what I see and I hear?

Volmar's serene face
furrows with care.
She sees the spirit in his eyes,
plucks opportunity
with boldness
dares write to an Emperor,
The Living Light advises you
be merciful.
Be aware of greed.
In your audacity, resist the devil's temptation.[41]

In an age of superstition
even a king trembles at her message.

Send for this holy lady.

Hildegard and Sister Inez
surrounded by armed soldiers,
colourful signature banners and torches
are escorted on the Roman Via Ausonia.
Inez sings their newest Latin poem
and together they find comfort and calmness
in the song of Divine Office.

Peasants group along the way
to see this *holy lady*, the healer.
Tillers in the field bow for blessing.
Children line the way, giggle and wave.

At Inglesheim Palace
bolstered by seeing a new world,
she stands before the King,
praises his restoration of Roman rule,
warns of antipopes, feudal violence,
abuse of power
then with a strident voice says,
*Listen O great one
it is the Living Light that speaks.*

Her voice quietens,
assumes a trance of authority,
I see a king
who fails to open his eyes,
and a dark haze comes,
which covers all the valley
and ravens and birds
tear bodies all around to pieces.
Hear this O King, make changes
if you wish to live.
Otherwise a sword will pierce you.[42]

He pales, a shadow clad in gold,
this so-called humble unlearned woman
warning him of greed!

Her words follow him, a thistle in his shoe.

Is it superstition or fear,
that makes King Barbarossa
grant her a charter of imperial protection?
All around his anger rains down.
Hildegard's abbey is left untouched.

VII
1158–1175

Hildegard emerged even further into public life, embarking on a series of preaching tours… Prophets 'illuminate the darkness…like the light of the sun. I felt the need to reach out to enkindle other hearts so that the imagination and creativity, forgiveness and contrition might flow again in the world.'
– Matthew Fox, *Illuminations of Hildegard of Bingen*

Three Missionary Journeys

Hildegard reminisces with Volmar and Clara
how the opportunities to speak out
still fill her with awe.
Her sixty-five-year-old eyes
come alive as she remembers
her missionary journeys.
Her face flushes
fear, excitement tingle again through her body.

Hildegard remembers the attention,
how her spine stiffened in response,
her voice switched onto a wave of authority,
soared like Bernard's eagle.
Bishops, clergy, monks listened.

She reminisces
how the speaking earthed her,
solid as the sandstone blocks
laid down for their new convent.
I spoke with an apocalyptic tone
as one with freedom of nothing to lose,
I did not hold back, like those
who fear repercussions.

She recalls the journey to Triers
her time in Metz, Wurzburg, Bamberg.

During her third tour,
on the steps of Cologne Cathedral
she admonished the prelates,
defiled by lust and adultery,
corrupted by greed,
buying and selling of holy office.
At my words their faces
turned the colour of boiled linen.
Hildegard smiles at Volmar,
rubs her aching knee, continues,
They backed away, tried to escape,
but the lay people pressed closer,
trapped them in.

She smiles, knowing
the papal recognition
of her writings as *Divinely inspired*,
silenced the superstitious,
disarmed the critics.

She shrugs at the hours on foot,
in the saddle, on boats.
Her tired body was relieved
by warm welcomes
in abbeys, convents along the way.
They called me their Mother.

Volmar interrupts,
No more my sister,
the journeys took their toll on you,
each time on your return,
your exhaustive collapse
was a worry, a concern.

She sits up, alert,
I knew the improbability of being heard.
Yet my call to repent and change
brought tears and smiles to many faces.
I also knew my blessings of hope and viriditas
would touch my people.

A Hum of Learning

The morning sings.
Through the Scriptorium window
the sun inches up.
Hildegard welcomes the light
for the day's work.
The room fragrant with a tang
of inks, wax and hide
embraces endeavour.

A wave of enthusiasm swells
as six sisters now familiar with Latin
copy liturgical music
for many commissions from convents.

The scriptorium hums with learning
to prepare and bind the quires.
Hildegard looks on, proud of their efforts.

The Divine Light in her mind's eye
plays its orbs of gold.
Writing cries to be done.
Volmar's quill awaits
and Hildegard's visions flow.
A new decade of writing begins.
Her third visionary work is born.[43]

Expansion to Eibingen

Hildegard's fingers tap restlessly
on the refectory table.
A new plan consumes her mind.
She moves to the podium,
tucks back some loose strands of grey hair,
smoothes her veil
waits for her sisters to end supper.

She looks around.
A hundred sisters sit close in lines
share their own produce,
freshly baked spelt bread,
honey, warmed grape wine.
Hildegard breathes the aroma
of the delicious broth,
a recipe she has created
for their health.

Her mind holds a bold horizon
as the shape of Rupertsberg
silhouettes into the sky.
Its soul is their singing, her music.

Hildegard inspires their hearts
again with the bravery of St Ursula.

Her voice lowers,
My gaze is drawn across the Rhine
to the hamlets and people of Eibingen,
to a destroyed, abandoned convent.
The local people beckon
for our sisters.

Chatter buzzes, hums
like a hive of Odelia's bees.
Excitement palpable.
They imagine the old buildings
brought to life again
by their efforts.

On the first Sunday of Lent
Hildegard crosses the busy Rhine
with thirty volunteer sisters
to found a new convent
amongst the people of Eibingen.
Sister Inez, chosen the new Magistra.

The monk Volmar comes to bless them.
Carpenters and stone masons follow
enthusiastic about a new project.

On the return journey,
the smell of the river captivates Hildegard.
Undeterred by the rough swell,
she turns to Volmar,
We will visit twice a week
to encourage and support them.

The buildings and spires of Rupertsberg
from the perspective of the Rhine
catch warm rays of a sun,
rest deep in their hearts.

Volmar

Volmar listens, eyes intense.
His quiet presence anchors her.
Their bond flows strong,
weathers shoals and unfamiliar currents.

He struggles to his feet,
grips a staff for support
presents a copy of her new work.

Hildegard swallows deeply.
Her temple twitches.
Shock shoots through her body.
It pains her to see him shuffle
his usual confident step slowed.
She sees suffering etched on his brow,
how his long black hair
has turned to tarnished silver.
They look at each other, say nothing.
Volmar nods.

Thoughts barely bearable flash into her mind.
How long do we have to finish our work?
Panic seizes her.
A cold draught shivers her neck,
busyness has camouflaged
the creep of time and Volmar's
six decades of stalwart presence.

My brother, freedom still eludes us.
We must write again. Demand control of our revenue.
Disibodenberg must release us
give us sovereignty.

He reassures her,
agrees to scribe her new letter
demanding release of their dowries.
His anxious eyes gaze kindly
as she sighs with relief.

Stand up for Freedom

Hildegard's head throbs.
Without control of their revenue
her Abbey and her sisters
are powerless.

Exhausted, she collapses,
finds refuge in her sickbed.

Guda's tender care,
thick spelt and turtle soup
comes with elderberry tea,
and the mulled wine for strength.
Always cheerful, Clara reads to her.
Hildegard hears her sisters singing
her canticles and antiphons.
Its sound rises to heaven
on the breath of angels.

Eyes half closed
she watches in candle glow
the slender figure of a new sister
serve her sustenance.
Hildegard recalls her young self
and feels renewed purpose.
Resolution floods
her weak limbs.
She will not give in
There is much to fight for.

She calls Clara to assist her
and goes back to her desk.

Volmar finds her writing on her tablet.
She presents her ideas, smiles wanly.
Here are my words to scribe.
I write for my sisters.

His words of comfort almost inaudible.
Together we will take up a last stand.

The Letter

To Helengerus, Abbot of Disibodenberg.
To you who have political advancement before God.

Not to release our dowries is unjust, selfish, illegal.
I can see you've ignited a black fire against Rupertsberg.
Yes I see this in you. I'm only a poor insignificant woman,
weak and worthless, yet if you listen to me,
you'll learn something.

Inside your soul, you must feel embarrassed
when you see yourself for who you are.
Sometimes you're an angry growling unkind bear,
but since you are so weak, you only snarl quietly under your breath.

Sometimes you're a reckless ass. Other times you're like certain birds,
which neither soar through the highest heights, nor hug the earth,
they neither excel, nor get in trouble. They're just apathetic and mediocre.

Finally in some affairs you're totally useless – your faithlessness
makes you spineless.

Here's what our omnipotent Father has to say:

I don't like your fickleness and your duplicity.
I don't like the way you snarl at My Justice.
I don't like the way you refuse My Wisdom
to solve your problems.
You nurse the pettiness inside you.
You shun God in your thoughts…
Be careful
for you know not when the sword will find you.[44]

Release of Dowries

Hildegard hears a drag of sandals.
Volmar enters the refectory,
his face aglow.

Let us give thanks.
A missive has come.
Revenue from your dowries to be released,
by order of the Bishop of Mainz.

Alleluia,
Hildegard stands up claps with delight.
Now we can manage our monies,
no longer at the behest of Disibodenberg.
Justice is done.
Rupertsberg is the Queen clothed in gold.[45]

The news at sext brings the church alive,
music rings a carillon of bells across the Rhine.

Hildegard hears her mind sing with joy,
Run, my daughter run,
for you have been granted wings.
Quickly, therefore, fly
over all these creatures opposing you
with comfort and release,
take up your wings, fly
over venomous and death-dealing vipers.[46]

Ripening

Summer gives way
to autumn mellowness.
Blush of dawn opens
softer skies, milder days.
Volmar draws up a rough map
notes places, people and tolls,
revenue from their dowries.

Hildegard and Volmar ride out
breathing confidence and zest.
It's a time of tumbling leaves,
abundance of fruit, grapes,
apples, wild plums, mulberries
quinces, hazels, chestnuts,
all for the picking.

She smells stench of malt, dye houses,
recoils at the reek of tanneries.
Her ears prick at clank of forges
mills and water wheels,
tune into the lilt of troubadours
and balladeers.
Her eyes feast on the bounty of markets.

Children follow them on the side.
Villagers stop and bow to receive
Hildegard's blessing.

Scattered tofts, sheepfolds in the distance,
gold of ripening fields, yoked oxen,
wayside husbandry, copses of osier,
dovecots, buzz of apiaries.

Hildegard holds the reins
Vision of the future buoys her.

At times she dismounts amongst the people
listens to their struggles, admires their vibrancy,
humbled by their loyalty.

On their return journey
Volmar smiles at Hildegard's excitement.

Now Rupertsberg is secure my sister.
See how the people love and care for you.

A serious frown crosses his face.
If I should die, bury me in our orchard,
he states matter-of-factly,
after more then twenty years
this is my home too.

Tears well in Hildegard's eyes
I will, my brother, I will.
Our abbey is indeed your home.

Felicity

After vespers,
Hildegard shares a new song.[47]
Her singing soars
into the heavens. Her sisters
stop to listen.
Hildegard gestures
to join in, harmonise,
O flower, you did not spring from the dew
nor from drops of rain,
nor did the air sweep over you,
but the Divine Radiance
brought you forth on a most noble branch[48]

The completed dome of their church
can barely contain the sound.
There is a freshness, a new power.
It stills their hearts
yet fires their Benedictine passion.
Their songs into silence,
a hush so heavy with rapture
they can scarcely breathe.
The moment holds them.
What has happened?
Something has touched them,
seized their senses.

Hildegard breaks the reverie,
gestures towards the walls.
Our murals are complete.
They mirror our song.
The sisters turn to look.
In the flicker of new beeswax candles
the walls glow with subtle colours.
Panelled frescos
tell the story St Ursula and her Virgins.
She hears a great communal breath,
watches the Spirit shine
in her sisters' faces,
as she inspires their monastic spirit
with the Ursuline journey.

Last Missionary Journey

Visitors' stories bombard her ears.
Rumours hit like truncheons.

It seems the Devil comes up
to meet her everywhere.
Thomas à Becket murdered at his altar,
a second bloody crusade, a third antipope.

Disillusion will not win,
Hildegard grits her teeth,
nor will pain and weakness.

She draws up her tired body,
shoulders heavy and curved,
sighs deeply,
prepares to journey once again.
She hoists her mantel over her arm,
shuts the door behind her.

A hesitant limp
betrays her determined step.
The Divine Light calls.
She must obey.

There is work to be done. She chooses two sisters to accompany her
smiles at their flighty excitement.
She frowns as the edge of pain assaults her body.
Compresses of steeped dried nettle
and comfrey bring some relief
but age and pain weigh on her.

She visualises herself in Swabia.
I must speak out against men, stiff-necked
with pride and arrogance.
Broilsome, contentious,
self-willed, guard dogs garnering
the world's worthless treasures.
Will they ever listen?
Hear how Ecclesia, our Mother, suffers.

She adds to Volmar,
I must journey forth in these dark times,
speak out for our people.
They especially need encouragement.

Passing of Volmar

In the dead of winter's beauty,
on a white frame of broody light,
hoarfrost spears hang.

From the hearth
crackle of wood-sage
sucks and spits.
Holy candles gasp for air.
Volmar's lips blue with chill.

Guda is alert to his every need,
her own face etched with time.
Her cousin Adelheid hovers.
Clara's rosy face cannot hide her desolation.

Hildegard wills the dimming sun to stay
but nothing will warm Volmar now.
He retreats before her unflinching gaze,
looks at her, without a word.
She clings to his ink-stained hand,
lays her head on his breast
until stillness.

Her face drains ashen.
She lets go of his hand.
The cry of an owl
cuts the silent air.

The sisters gaze in disbelief
as she covers his face,
Hildegard has run out of tears.
She struggles to breathe,
whispering,
orphaned,

She clasps her cloak
shawling the night about her.

An Obstinant Hierarchy

The sound of falling clods of clay
still thud in her ears.
She has buried Volmar in the orchard.
She has buried her companion, confidante,
her secretary, Provost for her two communities.

Abbot Helengerus,
the shadow of a raptor taunts her,
refuses to replace Volmar.
An ungraspable foehn wind howls injustice.

Do the hierarchy want me to sink into that hole,
to punish me, withhold
our sacramental needs?

Hildegard's razor-bone anger spurs.
Has she the strength to fight again
and without her stalwart Volmar?

As days pass
Her head throbs.
She cannot move.
Comforting presence comes
from her older blood sister Clementia
widowed and now a postulant.

And then the voice of Clara cuts the gloom,
Little mother don't fight it, grieve no longer.
The old monk, Gottfried is come,
our new provost.

News of Gottfried's arrival
takes its time to sink in.
She rises to welcome him.
Gottfried, slow and round and old,
an admirer, who aspires to be her hagiographer.
She finds him, tired and breathless
in the infirmary soaking his swollen feet,
sipping nettle tea,
cared for by a devoted cluster of her sisters.
Alleluia, she says, embracing him.
Our new provost and secretary.
Her face glows with a welcoming smile.
Her request answered.
Spiritual nourishment once more.

VIII
1176–1178

Fidelity

By fall Gottfried is dead,
just a year into his service.
The fiery Bishop Christian of Mainz
refuses to replace him.

Itinerant monks assist with the sacraments.
Clara tutors sisters
in the scriptorium.

Bishop Christian suns himself in Italy
and takes more interest
in being chancellor to Emperor Barbarossa
than being at home to his people.

I *will not have my sisters witness their Abbess
yield to such play of power again,*
Hildegard swears to Clara, in a hoarse voice.

She walks to and fro,
bereft at the ignorance and arrogance
of her beloved church.
Rage turns to defiance.
*We will bypass the bishop.
write directly to the Pope,
request he appoint a new provost.*

They await a papal reply.

Her sisters' singing gladdens her
as do almond trees that burst into bloom.
Faithful pilgrims are her balm.

At evening homily, her voice quivers
the way of the river on a windy day.

We stay faithful
in absence as in presence,
she reminds her sisters.

The hum of fruitfulness
in every corner of the abbey
is their response.

Guibert of Gembloux

Alleluia! Hildegard calls to Clara.
She brandishes a scroll bearing
the red seal of a papal directive.

We have permission
to override the local hierarchy.
I have invited
Guibert of Gembloux
to join our Abbey.

Clara swings onto her feet
clasps Hildegard's hands.

He will arrive in time for Easter.
We can prepare our liturgy and music
with renewed fervour.
I will get the postulants to make
fresh beeswax candles for the altar.

Hildegard creates a cosmic mandala[49]
for Sisters Bertrude and Agnes
to embroider on new vestments.
They sew stoles and chasubles
in Easter white and gold
for Guibert's welcome.

She sets out for Eibingen
her twice-weekly crossing of the Rhine.
It is joyful news she carries.

The ferrymen lift her gently into the boat.
Clara wraps cushions softened with fur pelts
and holds her still through the journey.
Hildegard's eyes embrace the patchwork cliffs
that hold faithful to the river.
She breathes its river-smells,
Oh how I love this river and its hills.

The rhythmic surge of oars
counters the current,
wild, windy, rough.
Hildegard undeterred
as they thread the traffic
of fishing boats and merchant craft.

Hospitality

A stranger staggers to the gate,
limps like a ship with torn, split sails.
Body dishevelled
stooped, hollow-cheeked,
in threadbare pilgrim garb.

His eyes, dulled with pain
come alive as he moans the name
Holy Hildegard.

Rumours spread,
sisters, pilgrims, workers
are aware of his presence.
From whence has he come?

Hildegard listens to his story
learns of his excommunication.
He confides his fear of dying.
Guibert takes his confession
blesses him.
He finds grace, begs to stay.

Benedictine hospitality says *Yes*
Church authority says *No.*
Hildegard reassures him.

He struggles from his bed
ashen, weak, his feet shuffle for balance.
He makes it to Sister Guda's herb garden,
helps pick and prepare leaves
and other herbs for the infirmary.

Within weeks he slips away.
Hildegard has him buried
in their cemetery
under the early bloom
of apple and pear tree.

Summer

Guibert finds Hildegard
in the cloister, a solitary figure.
She hears the rustle of his step, turns.

From the folds of his serge robe
he withdraws an open scroll.
A frown etches his brow.

My lady, he bows,
word from Mainz does not sound favourable.
There is anger at our decision of interment.

She shrugs. Breathes deeply.
It is done.
The man is blessed and buried.

She taps his arm to reassure him,
catches panic in his eyes.

Fear seizes Hildegard.
There is bad odour here.
The power-thirsty Bishop
could pounce, punish.
Her jaws clench.

Hildegard gathers herself.
The Divine Light is my authority
not the word of man.
Enough for now.

She shuffles away on her stick.
Guibert's frown deepens.

A Visit from the Canon of Mainz

In flowing red travelling robe
the bishop's toughest negotiator,
the canon of Mainz
alights from a horse-drawn carriage,
calls for fare.

In the chapter hall
Hildegard with Clara and Guibert take their place.
He folds his hands.
You risk the Bishop's wrath…

Anger courses through Hildegard.
She cuts in, her voice sharp
He had confessed and repented,
with barbs exposed she adds,
No sin so great that it is not worthy of forgiveness.

The canon clasps his hands
in an ironic guise of piety,
That man was an excommunicant.
You cannot break papal law.
The body must be exhumed.

Rage brings her to her feet.
Exhumed!

Yes, you must remove…it…from sacred ground.
he states with a dogmatic sweep.
He stands, stares her down.

Guibert's hands grip the bench,
swallows his dismay,
You…you ask us to dig up the body?

Hildegard's face burns crimson,
her breath comes in gasps.
We cannot exhume him.
If we are to heed the word of truth,
we cannot.
I will never move him.
she states with emphatic tone.

You…you…would refuse? He glares at Hildegard.

We refuse, she says.
Her head nods.
Her eyes burn into his.

He stands over her,
If you refuse, Archbishop Christian will impose
punishment on all the Abbey,
until you… his fingers jab pointedly at Hildegard
…until you…are obedient.
Your unruly way is not tolerated.

She stretches to her full height,
Tell the archbishop,
here at Rupertsberg Abbey
we obey God rather than man.

The canon steps back in shock,
I would remind you of St Paul's letter to Timothy,
Let the woman learn in silence…

Hildegard stands firm.
Through the roar of her blood,
with an angry shout
she mocks his words,
and suffer not a woman to teach
or to usurp authority over a man but to be in silence!

We will see who has the authority.
He speaks with a measured voice,
My men will remove the body.
Your punishment will come.

As the door clangs and chains rattle
her hands shake. She clutches the lectern.
Clara comes to help her to chapel for none.
Hildegard's steps witness to new pain.
After prayer she sits, shoulders slumped
discerns a plan only she can know
so only she can be blamed.

Somehow she will find the strength
to struggle out to the orchard
alone, after vespers.

She will disguise the burial plot.
The sisters cannot be asked to help.
This will be her doing.

Defiance

Clara finds Hildegard
cold,
mud-splattered.
An onslaught of questions
brings no response.

She helps Hildegard to her cell
in silence.
Tired, windy eyes and chaffed lips
betray the ache in her red swollen joints.
No herbal tea relieves her metallic taste.
Clara brings heated water-irons for her feet,
Bertrude's knitted muffs for her hands.
Guda brews a warming tea
of lemon balm and juniper leaves.

Whispering fears
of losing their abbess cloud the abbey.

In the light of a new day
Hildegard holds her counsel
with pursed lips.

Strength mustered in the cemetery
is spent,
yet she insists
on sharing the communal meal.
From her crafted carry-chair
she looks out at many anxious faces,
seeks to sustain her sisters,
listens intently to the readings.

In the chapel
after singing vespers
Hildegard stands
limps, holds onto pews
points at each fresco
as the journey of Ursula again unfolds.
The sisters follow with curious eyes.
They sing Ursula's hymns
seventy voices fired with courage.

All is Well

Horses in the courtyard.
Yelling in the orchard.
Silence fills the church.

Cold fear intrudes.
Hildegard shuffles with her staff to the altar,
her breath laboured.
She stands with Clara,
staring at the carved oak door.

The sisters cling to each other
huddle together,
wait
for a crash of entry.

Hildegard listens intently to the commotion.
She imagines the men's anger.
Crosses gone from the cemetery,
unable to fulfil their orders
– exhume the body.

With shouts and curses,
they gallop off to report their failure.
There will be consequences.

Sound of hoofbeat fades into the distance.
Silence.
Her plan has succeeded.

Hildegard glances around at her sisters.
Smiles her relief.
All is well.
They have gone.
It is over.

IX
1178–1179

Interdict

The archbishop circles.
Like a predator he smells her weakness.
To forbid the singing
will strangle her nourishment,
her abbey's lifeblood.
Disobedience
means destruction.

Wild storm of flint and hooves,
pounding rattles the gates.
Harsh strikes of the bell call all to the refectory.
Some younger sisters cringe and whimper.

A cleric in long black habit breaks
the red wax seal,
unfolds a scroll.
As if let off a chain
he snarls his attack.
This abbey is under an interdict
from Archbishop Christian of Mainz.
All sacraments and music are banned forthwith!

Hildegard raises her hand,
Enough.
She grabs the scroll, shouts at him and his entourage,
Get out!
Shock spasms down her spine.

Even as autumn dances on trees and garden
it is cold.
Even though the sun is terce high
it is dark.
Even though Presence surrounds her
she is lonely.

Without Song

Fugitive winter clouds
hold the sky ransom.
Low slant of sun
dims the chapel.

Whispered words of Divine Office
cloaks her sisters against the chill,
prepare them for their day's work.
How long?
How long can they live
without their music?

Unable to dispense the sacraments
Guibert presides at silent liturgy
prays alone in his quarters.

Days of gloom chill their hearts.
Curls of smoke from the village
spread a pall across the land.

As they work in the abbey
dark silhouetted hills shadow them,
like a mausoleum.
Hildegard's anger shows in her taut shoulders
and troubled eyes.

Struggle in Exile

Advent
casts deep sorrow.
It is cold, dark, silent.
Hildegard hears mumblings.
She reassures her sisters
with her presence at Rupertsberg,
her visits to Eibingen.

The darkest nights of the year
anticipate the fledgling Christ Light.
In the chapel candlelight
resolve flickers in her eyes.
Listen, listen, listen.
My sisters this is our time to listen.
As we pray the words
listen to their song in your hearts,
she continues,
The bishop cannot forbid us to listen.
Silencing the outer sound
does not silence us.
Search out the house of your heart.
Hope lies within.
She points to the fallowed gardens
blanketed by white-sleeted hay.
Contemplate its promise.
As silence in absence of bird-song
reminds us, music will return.

While the interdict diminishes them
mealtime together brings nourishment:
hot spelt bread, garden broths, teas
and from their harvest of stored foods,
bottled quince, the warmth of
herbs and hot berry wines.
They listen to the Nativity story.
Conversation swirls over the tables.

When the postulants, last season,
singing joyfully, picked purple sloes
and red hawthorn berries in the woods,
to brew and bottle,
little did they know the comfort,
their warm wines would be,
how perfect for this dark time.

Endurance

Snowbells, harbingers of spring
brave soldiers,
thrust up their tiny heads
into the imposed silence of Rupertsberg.

The trickle of pilgrims swells,
the Rhine quickens freckled with snow.
Peasants arrive eager to work.

For some sisters despondency rules,
hems drag in the dirt.
Some visit the infirmary
for valerian tea.

For Hildegard weight of reason
gives way to paradox
poetry and parable.
Let us find purpose in our day,
Hildegard counsels after matins,
find music in the fields
in the sun's warmth,
its glint of gold on boughs of the trees.
Rejoice in the aroma of the damp earth
and viriditas,
Spring is at the node of every greening branch.
May even the wind be our song.

Extra sisters work in the scriptorium.[50]
Clara, a shimmer in her voice,
proudly reports to Hildegard,
We have the best ink and parchments,
the new oil lanterns show off our efforts.
Many are keen and creative
in lettering, detail and decoration.
The Latin tutoring Inez gave
empowers us.

In the infirmary
with vigilance and careful observation,
Wilfredis keeps many sisters busy
and in the silence they learn,
in Hildegard's words,
to search out the house of their hearts.

My Quill, My Sabre

Hildegard sits,
slumps over her tablet
at her prie-dieu.

At terce she listens
to the rhythmic murmur
as her sisters whisper the Office,
lifts a determined chin.
Even now approaching eighty-one
her fight for justice will not cease.

Thoughts flow to her tablet.
Volmar, I miss you.
In five years without you,
justice has not been served.
I have to write again.
I need your strength.
Like a river I am turned off course.
My life flows into another channel.
I am lost.
I do not recognise my shores.

Her throat tightens,
she feels her burden settle.

We are exiles in our own abbey, our home.
Exiled from our life's work of sung praise.
Exiled from spiritual nourishment.
Exiled from our meaning.
Will we, like the elderberry plants
that struggle at the edge of the woods,
deprived of nourishment
wither and die?

Is this what they want of our abbey?

Her breath quickens.
She will not die now.
Is it this great trial keeps me alive?
Is my life inexhaustible?

Through the choke of a silent scream
she pounds the prie-dieu with her fist.
Damn these prelates.
This punitive silence is demonic.
Only the devil can stop music.

I cannot drag these old bones
through the countryside
to beg for yet another audience.
I will not be silent
I will be heard

One more letter!
My quill will be my sabre.
I sharpen it for a final battle.

The Final Letter

Letter to Archbishop Christian of Mainz

Words come to me. In my soul the Light of a Great Vision
the corpse here in our blessed ground must never be removed.
To do so would be contrary to the Will of the Truth.

Lest we appear to be disobedient we have followed the ban,
have suspended the singing of the Divine Office
and the reception of Sacrament. My sisters and myself
have experienced great sorrow.

We are fettered, bound by you, our superiors, prelates
and honourable men who demand our disobedience to the True Light
a maze that holds us powerless.

Whilst I and all my sisters are afflicted with great bitterness
and oppressed by huge sadness…
we have obeyed.

I heard a voice from the Living Light
tell of what David says in the psalms:
Give praise in the call of the trumpet,
praise on the psaltery and lute,
praise on the tambour and in dancing,
praise on strings and harp,
praise on resonant cymbals,
praise of jubilation.
Let every spirit give praise.

*It is Satan who hears man sing
through Divine inspiration,
and it is Satan who constantly works to destroy
this beauty of Divine Praise and Hymnals of Spirit.*

*So you and all prelates must use the greatest vigilance
in stopping, by decree, the mouth of any assembly
of people singing to God.
Beware,
lest in your judgement you are ensnared by Satan,
who draws man out of the celestial harmony
and the delights of paradise.*

*By silencing song in our abbeys you cut human fellowship
with the angelic praise of heaven, but graver still
you disrupt the harmony of body and soul.*[51]

The Long Silence

A year of testing.
Hildegard has obeyed.
Now she has challenged.

With trembling hands
she opens the reply to her emissive.

Her letter serves its purpose.
The interdict is lifted.
Fear of damnation
and accusation
of siding with the devil
has jolted the bishop's guilt.

Clara rings the bell.
It echoes around the abbey
as if the sky sings.
The sisters gather in great jubilation
to hear the letter
and softly, tentatively, sing the office.

It is a time full of promise
brimming with skylarks.
Spring overflows
into every corner of the abbey.
The last week of Lent
has never been more hopeful.

At the lenten mealtimes
even though a strict fast
sisters beam in great joy.
Paschal feast of Easter is imminent.
They will once again
sing and dance and celebrate.

Her Last River Journey

Clara, I must go to Eibingen
I need to inform our dear Inez
and her sisters.

Little mother there is no need.
We will go.

I wish for the journey.
It will be my Easter blessing
and farewell to my sisters.
We will sing together one last time
My hymns to St Ursula will give Inez
renewed hope and courage.

It was one of those late spring days
a prelude of season's change,
a day to reflect and savour.
A time of in-betweens
as earth turns and yields.

It is Hildegard's last river crossing.
Every bone hurts.
No amount of cushioning
can bring protection
from surging current.
The porters carry her proudly.
There is a muted hush
as their *holy lady* goes by.

Lines of people bow, she blesses them.
Many eyes are filled with tears.
Children wave, awed to quietness.
The oarsmen bow humbly.

Banks awash with half-thawed snow
mean a frisky river.
Spring rain stings her face.
Ice-melting wind
rips at her breath.
Waves toss her boat. Ferrymen
mumble apologies.

On the Eibingen bank
people hush and kneel
as *their Mother*, Hildegard
is lifted from the boat.

They sing the Mass and Divine Office.
So much music, so much joy.
Candle glow on her sisters' faces
reassures Hildegard.

She wonders,
how can my eyes so worn
be still so eager, hungry
for still more light?

My soul magnifies the Lord,
they sing with angelic voices,
I am the Resurrection and the Life.

As the visitation ends
Inez reaches out to Hildegard.
Tears rest on her drawn face,
Hildegard strokes her cheek.

You have the music, my dear sister.
You and your sisters give much,
you will receive much.
You have the strength –
strength in love.
It is all about life and living to the full.
The music gives wings
your gift to each other.

They exchange a loving glance
and one long embrace.

Hildegard looks at Clara and Guibert
as the Rhine River carries them back.
Oh how I will miss this river,
its fresh smell, its lull,
its reeds and colour.

As she journeys back
up the hill to Rupertsberg
Hildegard's eyes fill with love,
a last look on her people,
out over her beloved Rhineland.

Much Joy, Much Pain

Time slows. Hildegard sees
everything in slow motion.
Leaden grief lifts.
Her soul soars,
spirals into golden orbs of Light.
Her heart rejoices
yet aches for her sisters.
In the beauty of the Cosmos
she sees so much pain
piercing the centre of the Cross.
For Hildegard, aged and infirm
music and pain arc as one.

Shafts of light
with their chameleon pastels
linger.

For her, there are no words.
In the silence
the beauty of her internal landscape
catches her heart,
frees her spirit.

Last Days

Autumn stirs.
Aroma of pickles zings from the kitchen.
Sisters carry Hildegard to the chapel.
She sits nested, cushioned into her chair.

They wait silently,
drink in her every word.
Her homilies transfix
with faint voice
her eyes shine with light.
Let us be alive,
burning offerings
before the altar of our Creator.

Live with the moistness of passion.
if you lack the verdancy of Justice
your soul is dry.
Viriditas,
she whispers,
viriditas,
it is your healing.
Love the fecundity of life.
Let all who are thirsty come.[52]
Be ablaze with enthusiasm.

She reminisces as she shares,
smells the sweet damp woods
she ran through as a child,
hears the childhood brook
clinking its pebbles along.
She speaks of ferns and flowers and stones,
the interconnection of all things.
There is no creation that does not have a radiance,
be it greenness or seed, blossom or beauty,
it could not be creation without it.[53]

Hildegard's Song

Autumn deepens.
Lone deciduous trees
glow muted yellow
among the pine forests.

Afternoon light
burns wine-red
on the vineyard-clad mountain,
its slant of sun shortening
as it prepares to leave.

Dawn mist shrouds the Nahr,
lifts with a sense of melancholy.

Hildegard's song
sings deeper and deeper in her heart.
The more silent she is, the closer the music.
It could be her sisters in chapel
singing louder for her,
or just her heart in song.

After vespers her sisters
come to her.
She blesses each in turn.

The end comes dimly,
she senses the light's darkness,
close and holy.
She welcomes this land now
hears it fall, note by note upon her heart
craving its rest.

A Circle Ends Where it Begins

Night sounds. Bird chatter calms
as they settle to roost. Frogs and crickets
interrupted by the near-by cry of an owl.

Whispers call Hildegard.
The bee lured to the open armed flower.

Into her room a moon tucks in,
plays warm shadows
on the faces gathered around her.
Hildegard sees a celestial choir
singing the Mass and Office
with Guibert as their priest.

The scent of roses fills the air.
She remembers the smell
of Richardis's perfumed hands
bringing her a flush of roses
that initial year at Rupertsberg.

In her dreams she sees a loving Jutta
calling her to instruct Richardis
on gathering plants for balms.
Remembers how they ran hand in hand
into the forest
curious about ferns,
flowers, stones, seeds and berries.

She sees Volmar's warm eyes.
Rides with him from Disibodenberg,
hears again his words,
I could not let you go alone.

She sees a young girl,
vigorous as a blossom in full bloom.
She runs in breathless,
Jutta, O Jutta
she calls,
I see the light and beyond to the heavens.
I want to express myself so much.
I feel so blessed.

She watches the young girl pluck a feather
from under her coarse homespun cape,
and look, a gift.
I know there are always feathers,
but this was special, as I watched it drift.
I felt a 'Yes' to life.
Ah, I am a feather on the breath of God.

Hildegard watches herself both hands in the air,
eyes to the heavens, turn and twirl a dance of light.

Epilogue

> Let us go out early to the vineyard,
> and see whether the vines have budded,
> whether the grape blossoms have opened
> and the pomegranates are in bloom.
> There I will give you my love.
> – Song of Songs 7:12

It was the monk Guibert who sat with the new abbess Clara and the magistra Inez from Eibingen and documented Hildegard's life after she died on 17 September 1179. They collected the writings of the old monk Gottfried who wanted to be her hagiographer.

It was the sisters who collected and collated Hildegard's writing and compositions. When Guibert was called back to his monastery, the monk Theoderic put together the work and expounded on it.

The pilgrims who came, came to pray to their Saint Hildegard. The people made her a saint. They made pilgrimages to Rupertsberg Abbey. Many healings were reported and at harvest time they were blessed with the miracle of bountiful harvests and wonderful wine. The villagers said she was with them.

In 2012, nearly 900 years later, Saint Hildegard was officially canonised as a saint and made one of the four women Doctors of the Church.

Chronology

1098   Hildegard born in Bermersheim, to a lower-rank noble family, the tenth and last child.

1099   The First Crusade.

1101   Hildegard reports visionary experiences from age three.

1106   Hildegard placed in the care of Jutta of Sponheim from a noble family (a tithe to the Church). Later on, she will forbid young children be given to the Church.

1112   Jutta and Hildegard enter an anchorage attached to the monastery at Disibodenberg. As anchorites, they are under the authority of Abbot Kuno.

1120   Volmar (a young monk and academic at Disibodenberg) is appointed as Hildegard's confessor.

1124   Richardis von Stade born.

1132   Richardis von Stade from a noble family and her cousin Guda are placed into the care of their Aunt Jutta to be educated in the convent. Her mother the Marchioness von Stade makes substantial donations to Disibodenberg and later at Rupertsberg.

1136   Jutta dies. Hildegard becomes the new magistra at 38 years of age. The anchorage has by this time grown into a small Benedictine convent (10 sisters).

1139   Hildegard discerns that she is called to write. She is refused permission by Abbot Kuno. Her health is poor (maybe migraines – a modern diagnosis). See Hildegard and Oliver Sacks, and Hildegard and Carl Jung.

1141   Hildegard has a fiery vision commanding her to write down what she sees and hears. More ill health. Finally, Abbot Kuno allows Volmar to scribe for Hildegard. At 42 years and 10 months, Hildegard begins her writings. Her first book called *Scivias* (The Way). This first major theological and visionary work takes ten years to complete.

1145 Pope Eugenius III, friend and student of Bernard of Clairvaux takes office (1145–1153).

1147 Hildegard writes to Bernard of Clairvaux seeking validation of her visions and writings. He takes them to the Pope. Her first letters date from this time.

The Second Crusade.

At the Synod of Trier, Pope Eugenius III authorises Hildegard's writings to continue. Papal approval acknowledges the Divine authority of her writing as Divinely inspired.

1148 Her musical compositions, the beginning of the *Symphonia* allowed and sung at the Monastery.

1149 Hildegard, now 50 years of age, asks to move her convent to the ruins of the old St Rupert's hermitage at Rupertsberg at the fork of the Rhine and Nahr Rivers. She is refused permission. Abbot Kuno improves the space for her sisters including a new convent. More ill health.

1150 The bishop demands she be able to move her convent for he fears if she dies her writing from God would not be complete. In response to the bishop's demand, Abbot Kuno allows her to go, but withholds the sisters dowries and keeps her under his authority.

Hildegard founds her first abbey at Rupertsberg. near the village of Bingen. (A 14th-century engraving that has survived shows an abbey of substantial size.) There were about 25 sisters. Volmar defies his abbot and accompanies Hildegard as her provost.

1151 *Scivias* completed. It describes in detail 26 visions, created, scribed and painted by Hildegard, Volmar and Richardis. *Scivias* finishes with her first version of the famous morality play, *Ordo Virtutum* (The Play of Virtues).

1152 At the blessing and dedication of her church, her

sisters perform her play *Ordo Virtutum*. All are invited, including Richardis's mother, the Marchioness of Stade and her son the bishop of Bremen.

Sister Richardis is commanded by her mother to leave and become abbess of a convent at Bassum that her brother the bishop has acquired for her.

Hildegard distraught, vigorously opposes the move. She accuses them of simony.

Hildegard feels the loss. No amount of letter-writing and demands bring Richardis back.

1153 News of Richardis's death (in her late twenties) reaches Rupertsberg the following year.

1153 Pope Eugenius dies.

Bernard of Clairvaux dies.

1154 Henry II becomes King of England. (Eleanor of Aquitaine, his wife, is among Hildegard's correspondents.) Hildegard, with Volmar as scribe, writes prolifically.

Hildegard begins writing two major medical treatises, the first on healing with nature, *Physica*, and the second, *Causae et Curae*, which studies the use of natural ingredients in diet and therapy to alleviate pain and to foster healing. They give insights into human physiology and pathology.

1155 Barbarossa crowned Holy Roman Emperor. Hildegard writes to him as a prophet. He summons her to the palace. Barbarossa extends an order of protection over the holy woman and her abbeys. Abbot Kuno dies. Abbot Helengerus replaces him.

1158 Hildegard's second visionary book, *The Book of Life's Merits*, is completed.

1158–62 Some dowries are received. Building projects at Rupertsberg are more affordable.

Hildegard's first missionary journey. She preaches at

monasteries as well as publicly, despite poor health and her busy ministry to pilgrims, to her sisters and her abbey.

Archbishop Arnold of Mainz officially recognises Rupertsberg Convent as a Benedictine abbey and Hildegard as abbess.

1160   Hildegard's second missionary journey. Barbarossa supports a series of antipopes.

1161   Hildegard's third missionary journey. She preaches at Cologne Cathedral to the clergy and lay people.

1163   Hildegard begins her third visionary book, *The Book of Divine Works*. Her correspondence grows. Begins to gather her music and songs into a bound manuscript, *The Symphony of the Harmony of Celestial Revelations*. Many convents and monasteries ask for her music, especially the antiphons for the Divine Office.

1165   Hildegard's abbey has flourished with over 100 sisters. Pilgrims come as word spreads of Holy Hildegard.

Hildegard founds her second abbey at Eibingen, across the Rhine from Rupertsberg and Bingen and above the town of Rudesheim. Hildegard crosses the Rhine twice a week to be with her Eibingen sisters.

1170   Thomas à Becket is murdered at Canterbury Cathedral in England. Despite poor health, Hildegard makes her fourth missionary journey. Hildegard writes the *Vita of St Disibod*, composes music for St Ursula and writes *Vita of St Ursula*.

1173   *The Book of Divine Works* is completed.

Volmar – Hildegard's confidant, secretary/scribe, confessor and long-term friend – dies.

Hildegard corresponds with a Belgian monk called Guibert of Gembloux. She sends him her writings and music.

1174 After much resistance from the new abbot, Helengerus at Disibodenberg, the old monk Gottfried is appointed as Volmar's replacement and begins to write Hildegard's *Vita*.

1175 Gottfried dies. The abbot at Disibodenberg makes it hard to replace him.

Hildegard writes to the Pope for help as her abbey needs a provost and secretary.

1176 The old monk Guibert of Gembloux becomes Hildegard's secretary and continues writing her *Vita*.

1178 Archbishop Christian of Mainz, the Chancellor to Barbarossa, issues an interdict against the abbey of Rupertsberg. Music is forbidden and liturgy restricted. The issue is the alleged burial of an excommunicant in the consecrated grounds of the Rupertsberg Abbey. They obey the interdict for nearly a year. Hildegard writes a long letter to the archbishop reminding him, only the Devil silences music. It was a seven-page manuscript which scholars today praise as an excellent 12th-century precis on music.

1179 April: interdict is lifted by the archbishop of Mainz in time for Easter.

17 September: Hildegard dies at Rupertsberg, age 82.

1186 Theoderic of Echternach finishes the first *Vita of Hildegard*.

Theoderic responsible for the second and third books of her *Vita* and their prefaces.

After 1200, Hildegard was declared a saint by the people. There are four attempts to have her canonised. They fail.

1600 Hildegard's name added to the Roman martyrology.

2012 Hildegard canonised and given status as Doctor of the Church.

Glossary

Abelard, Peter, 1079–1142 – medieval French philosopher, theologian, known for love of Heloise, whose work was silenced.

Apotheka or apothecary – a room where medicines are formulated and dispensed.

Aspirant – the first stage of religious life.

Anchoress – a woman who for religious reasons withdraws from secular society.

Anchorage – austere accommodation usually attached to a church or monastery with three openings: 1. opens into the church to receive communion called a squint; 2. allows assistants to deliver food and goods and exchange refuse; 3. opens to the street for people seeking wisdom, advice and prayers.

Antiphon – brief text from Gospels, sung before and after the psalm in terms of the day's feast in order to interpret it.

Ascetic – a person who follows severe self-discipline.

Barbarossa, Frederick, 1122–1190 – King of Germany and Holy Roman Emperor.

Bassum – monastery in the diocese of Bremen where Richardis of Stade was appointed Abbess.

Benedictine Order – monastic way of life with a daily pattern based on three pillars, prayer, work and study divided into the eight hours of space for the Divine Office. It is based on the Rule written by St Benedict in the fourth century.

Bermersheim – a wine-growing town in the Rhineland valley where Hildegard was born the 10th child of a noble family in 1098 and probably lived there till she was eight years old when she went to Sponheim Castle to live in community with Jutta (aspiring to be a religious at the time).

Bingen – an important river town on the Rhine River.

Canticles – songs in Divine Office usually from Old Testament.

Crusades – a series of medieval military expeditions made by Europeans to recover the Holy Land from the Muslims in the 11th and 12th centuries. Sometimes ironically called the Holy Wars. Hildegard lived in the time of the second crusade, which was preached by St Bernard of Clairvaux

Compline – see Divine Office.

Cumdach – a case used as a reliquary to store, enshrine or display manuscripts.

Disibodenberg – a Benedictine monastery 39 kilometres from Bingen at the confluence of the Nahr and Glan Rivers. It was founded by a hermit called St Disibod, who came as a missionary from Ireland in AD 640. Hildegard lived there for thirty-eight years.

Divine Office – the Liturgy of the Hours or Divine Office marks the hours of the day with prayer. Every three hours the Benedictines stop for prayer: matins – early morning; lauds – dawn; prime – morning; terce – 9 a.m.; sext – noon; none – 3 p.m.; vespers – dusk; compline – before bed.

Divine revelation – words and visions not from authority of reason and learning but rather received in and by grace.

Eibingen – a daughter convent across the Rhine River near Rudisheim. Founded by Hildegard in 1165. It was bombed at some stage but the parish church stands there today. with a large mosaic of the Blue Man (Trinity Mandala) above the altar.

Eleanor – a correspondent of Hildegard, spouse of Henry II. Eleanor died in 1204, her eighty-third year.

Fiefdom – a central element of feudalism. Workers held property rights in return for allegiance and labour.

Garth – an open space surrounded by cloisters; can include a garden.

Hagiographer – a writer of the life of a holy person.

Heretic – a baptised church member who rejects some laws, rules, or dogma of the church.

Interdict – an ecclesiastic censure or ban that prohibits persons from certain church activity.

Infirmary – a place where sick or injured people are cared for, a sick house in an institution.

Lauds – see Divine Office.

Lent – This is forty days of fast and penance from Ash Wednesday to the Paschal feast of Easter.

Magistra – a medieval Latin term of academic rank indicating role of teacher.

Matins – see Divine Office; means the morning song of birds.

Music – Hildegard's compositions (seventy-seven sacred songs, and a liturgical opera set to music) are unique, unlike plainchant and Gregorian chant. It is an original and new sound. Her sisters sang her music in the Divine Office eight times a day, especially on feast days.

None – see Divine Office.

Oblate – a person dedicated to a religious order.

Ordo Virtutum – an allegorical morality play or liturgical drama written and composed by Hildegard in 1151. Also referred to as an opera.

Pentecost – celebration of the coming of the Holy Spirit to the Apostles and Disciples, fifty days after Easter.

Psalter – the book of psalms for liturgical use.

Psaltery – a stringed instrument of the zither family. Played by plucking the strings.

Prie-dieu – a kneeling bench used by a person at prayer with a low armless upholstered chair and high straight back.

Prime – see Divine Office.

Provost – the head of a Christian community (historic meaning); today head of an institution.

Quire – four sheets of paper or parchment folded to form eight leaves, as in medieval manuscripts.

Rupertsberg – a twelfth century Benedictine Abbey on the Rhine River at Bingen. It was founded by Hildegard in 1150 – on the ruins of the eighth century Hermitage of St Rupert. Hildegard died and was buried there in 1179.

School of Chartres – an important centre of scholarship during eleventh and twelfth centuries. Artisans who came to work at Rupertsberg brought not only skills but ideas, writings, drawings and knowledge from Chartres.

Scriptorium – literally a 'place for writing'. A room in medieval European monasteries devoted to writing, copying and illuminating of manuscripts by monastic scribes and artists.

***Scivias* (Know the Way)** – Hildegard's first major visionary work, 1141–1151. The famous copy of *Scivias* was lost in 1945. However, the text and artwork are preserved in copies and a colour facsimile Two more visionary works followed over the next twenty years. One copy was taken to Dresden for safe keeping but was lost in the bombings of 1945. See Writings.

Seer – a person of supernatural insight.

Simony – buying and selling of church privileges and positions, Hildegard saw it as corruption.

Sext – see Divine Office.

Sponheim – castle and estate founded in eleventh century; the home of the Stade Family from which Jutta comes, hence her title Jutta von Sponheim.

Squint – the small opening from the anchorage to the chapel to receive Communion.

Terce – see Divine Office.

Thurible – a metal censer suspended from chains, in which incense is burned during service.

Timaeus – Plato's work on cosmology known in twelfth century by the translation by Chalcidius.

Thomas à Becket – chancellor under King Henry II. Resigned to become Archbishop of Canterbury, murdered at his altar in 1170 by the king's men.

Tithe – a contribution to a church or religious organisation. Hildegard being the tenth child, it was a tradition to offer her into the care of the church.

Trier – an early Roman town in Germany. It is noted for the cathedral of Trier, where Pope Eugenius affirmed Hildegard's writings.

Ursula – the legend of the martyred Saint Ursula and her 11,000 virgins has kept a global audience intrigued for centuries. Hildegard wrote poetry and many chants in honour of St Ursula. Her story painted as murals in church an inspiration for the sisters.

Vespers – see Divine Office.

Viriditas – a word coined and made famous by Hildegard. The word combines the essence of truth and green, meaning vitality, fecundity, lushness, verdure and growth. Hildegard uses it metaphorically as vitality. She sees it in the moist fresh growth. In her writings, *Viriditas* means the 'greening power of God'.

Vita – means the written life of a person by a designated author.

Wax tablet – a tablet made of wood and covered with a layer of wax. It was used by Hildegard as a reusable writing surface.

Woad – a flowering plant from which a blue dye is produced from its leaves to prepare ink.

Writings – Hildegard's creative output is staggering, even by modern, computer-day standards. In addition to the three visionary books – *Scivias* (Know the Way); *Liber Vitae Meritorum* (The Book of Life's Merits), 1151–1158; *Liber Divinorum Operum* (The Book of Divine Works), 1163–1173 – the sung morality opera, *Ordo Virtutum*, the two medical treatises on plants, health and healing – *Physica* and *Causae and Curae* – and ever-growing volume of correspondence, she composed seventy-seven liturgical songs and *Vitae* (Lives) of St Rupert, St Disibod and St Ursula.

Notes

A Poetic Journey seeks a middle ground between an accurate scholarly presentation of Hildegard and a personal interpretation of her story. I rely mainly on secondary sources with respect to references, dialogue and her richly worded insights. Others have had the skill to translate her writings from the Latin texts, from German and her early German dialect, and I respect and thank them.

The following references are noted in good faith. Hildegard's words are expressed in poetic form and in italics in the poetry. The integrity of the meaning and intent are in line with the sources consulted. Dialogue without footnotes is intuited from my reading and research

Prologue and 1
The dialogue is imagined.

II

1. Gabriele Uhlein, *Meditations with Hildegard of Bingen* (Santa Fe, 1982), hereafter abbreviated *Uhlein*, p. 90.
2. *Scivias* by Hildegard of Bingen, translated by Columba Hart & Jane Bishop (Paulist Press, 1990), hereafter abbreviated H&B), p. 18.
3. Matthew Fox, *Illuminations of Hildegard of Bingen*, (Santa Fe Bear & Co, 1985), hereafter abbreviated *Fox*, p. 36.
4. *Uhlein*, p. 9.
5. *Scivias*, pp. 3ff., 5, translated in Fox, p. 24.
6. Carmen Acevedo Butcher, *St Hildegard of Bingen: Doctor of the Church (*Paraclete Press, 2013). hereafter abbreviated *CB*, p. 63.

III

7. Medical books from Hippocrates and other Greek texts are said to have been widely available in the 12th century.
8. Psalm 36 adapted for a feminist theology.
9. On 22 December 1136, Jutta of Sponheim died at the age of 44 years at Disibodenberg.

Hildegard was bereft, left without her mother, called to become magistra. Later she would write, 'God infused this woman with his grace like a river of many waters so that she gave her body no respite, with vigils, fasts and other good works, until she crowned the present life with a good death.'
10. Hildegard of Bingen interpretation of Proverbs 8, cited in *CB*, p. 53.
11. Hildegard basically challenged this position. In her writings on essential wholeness of Divine creation, Hildegard refused to separate life which later is termed dualism into neat but useless categories of earth and heaven, body and soul, nature and human. *CB*, p. 160.

IV

12. Barbara Newman, *Symphonia, No.2, Sapentia* literature backgrounds this text (Ithaca 1998, The wisdom of Solomon and Ecclesiasticus 24:5–6).
13. *Fox*, p. 28.
14. 1 Timothy 2:12.
15. The appearance of the eagle in Hildegard's writings is a spur to awake and rise up seeking the Word of the Light. *Hildegard of Bingen, Selected Writings*, translated by Mark Atherton (Penguin Classics, 2001 (hereafter abbreviated *MA*), p. 208.
16. H&B, p. 59.
17. A vision of Hildegard, *MA*, pp. 3–4.
18. Jospeh Baird *Personal Correspondence of Hildegard of Bingen* (OUP 2004), hereafter abbreviated *JB*, letter to Bernard of Clairvaux.
19. *Scivias* by Hildegard of Bingen, H&B p. 112. This is a claim Hildegard makes quite often – to show her words are not of her tutoring but from the Divine Light.
20 *JB,* cited in Hildegard's letter to Bernard of Clairvaux.
21. *Fox*, p. 9.
22. Reply from the monk Bernard. It could be said the stars align for Hildegard. Hildegard in a dream is inspired to write to Bernard. Pope Eugenius is Bernard's protégé. Things fall into place for her. The papal envoy declares her words inspired. At the coming Synod of Triers the Pope reads and praises her writings. Hildegard, a woman, is given a path forward.

23. *The Rule of St Benedict*, Prologue.
24. *MA,* from Song for Saint Disibod an Irish monk and hermit, first mentioned in a martyrology by Hrabanus Maurus (AD 780–856). Hildegard wrote the lyrics and music for several songs to send to Disibodenberg at the request of the abbot and around 1170 she wrote the *Vita of Saint Disibod.*

V

25 'Hail O Greenest Branch' a hymn that sings of Mary as the branch of Jesse. Mary's fertility brings humanity to God through the joy of contemplating the Divine.
26. *Fox,* p. 36.
27. Romans 13:1 2–14.
28. Much is written on theory of Hildegard's music with a range of two and a half octaves with sense and breath of ecstasy.
29. *Ordo Virtutum (Order of the Virtues)* is an allegorical morality play, or liturgical drama, by Hildegard, composed c. 1151, translated by Linda Marie Zaer. It is the earliest morality play by more than a century, and the only Medieval musical drama to survive with an attribution for both the text and the music.

VI

30. *CB,* letter to Marchioness von Stade, p. 101.
31 *MA,* letter to Henry Bishop of Mainz, p. 51.
32. Barbara Lachman, *The Journal of Hildegard of Bingen,* letter in answer to the Bishop of Mainz, pp. 52–3. It is hard to assess the subjective effects of the warnings and threats with which Hildegard peppers her letters. There was shock tactic in her words, but it never actually worked to change the situation. In the main confrontations she won, there was usually some other factor to strengthen her claims. Often it was manifestation of illness as in case of the financial settlement at Disibodenberg and the move to her new abbey in Rupertsberg.
33. *MA,* letter to Richardis, p. 52.
34. Two books, *Physica* and *Causae et Curae,* followed that gave new understanding of human body, disease and medicinal cures till new breakthroughs of sixteenth century. Hildegard has access

to translated texts of Galen, a Greek physician, surgeon and philosopher AD 130–210 and other Greek medical books Volmar had acquired, also a female anatomy textbook from the Italian library of Trotula of Salerno. How much she could read we do not know, but she took them in. Hildegard's medical detailed writings were radical enough in the twelfth century Germany to shock religious men as well as scientific circles.

35. Dr Wighard Strehlow & Gottfried Hertzka, *Hildegard of Bingen Medicine*. trans Karin Strehlow (Bear & Co. 1988), p. 142.
36. *Fox*, p. 16.
37. Ibid., p. 48, Hildegard adaptation of Genesis 4:12.
38. Several weeks later, a letter from Richardis's brother, Hartwig, Archbishop of Bremen, a letter gave her the answer, '…Thus I ask as earnestly as I can, if I have any right to ask, that you love her as much as she loved you, and if she appeared to have any fault – which indeed was mine, not hers – at least have regard for the tears that she shed for your cloister, which many witnessed. And if death had not prevented, she would have come to you as soon as she was able to get permission. But since death did intervene…'
39. *CB*, letter to Henry King of England, p. 107.
40. Ibid., letter to Eleanor Queen of England and wife of King Henry II, p. 106.
41. Ibid., letters to Barbarossa pp. 102–103.
42. Cited as a letter, here adapted for dialogue. Christian Schuller, Bettina Kroker, Dr Matthias Schmundt, *Research on correspondence between Hildegard and Barbarossa*, landderhildegard.de

VII

43. *Liber Divinorum Operum* known as *The Book of Divine Works*. The first two visionary works being *Scivias* and *The Book of Life's Merits*.
44. *CB*, letter to Abbot Helengerus (Kuno's successor at Disibodenberg) 1170, p. 114.
45. Psalm 45.2.
46. *MA*, p. 44.
47. Hildegard was not being metaphorical when she called her music 'a new song' The monks chant for all

her formative years is grey and bland compared with her octave jumps, her word painting in music, lyrical leaps and lack of rules. She blamed it on 'being unschooled'.

48. *MA,* from *Ordo Virtutum.*

VIII

49. The comic mandala is a vision in her third visionary work DOD. The tree is the symbol of the cosmos. we see the cultivation of the earth through the seasons of the year and the seasons of our life.

IX

50. Many scribe and illumine beautiful, small books of the Benedictine Rule, or the Divine Office for Convents, on commission, Some copy the music for convents and other borrowed books for their library.
51. *CB*, adapted from letter to the prelates at Mainz. Scholars have praised the full letter as an excellent precise on the meaning and importance of music of the 12th century with relevance to today.
52. Isaiah 55:1.
53. Concept adapted from Barbara Lachman, *The Journal of Hildegard of Bingen*, Inspired by a year in the life of the twelfth-century mystic. Bell Tower, 1993.

Bibliography

Works consulted

Anderson, Bonnie & Zinsser, Judith, *A History of their Own; Women in Europe.* Perennial, 1988.

Bobko Jane, comp. and ed., *Vision: The Life and Music of Hildegard von Bingen.* Text by Barbara Newman, commentary by Matthew Fox.

Bowie, Fiona and Oliver Davies eds, *Hildegard of Bingen: An Anthology.* , SPCK 1990

Butcher, Carmen Acevedo, *St Hildegard of Bingen: Doctor of the Church.* Paraclete Press, 2013.

Cameron, Christine *Leadership as a Call to Service. Life & works of Hildegard of Bingen.* Connor Court, 2015.

Durka, Gloria, *Praying with Hildegard of Bingen.* Saint Mary's Press, 1991.

Fournier-Rosset, Jany, *From Saint Hildegard's Kitchen, Foods of Health, Foods of Joy.* Liguori, 2010.

Fox, Matthew, *Original Blessing.* Bear & Company, 1983.

Fox, Matthew, *Illuminations of Hildegard of Bingen.* Bear & Company, 1985.

Fox, Matthew, *Hildegard of Bingen A Saint for our Times.* Namaste, 2012.

Gottfried and Theoderic, Monks, *The Life of the Holy Hildegard.* Liturgical Press, 1980.

Heer, Friedrich, *The Medieval World, A Mentor Book,* 1962.

Hildegard of Bingen, *Scivias, The Classics of Western Spirituality,* trans. Mother Columba Hart and Jane Bishop. Paulist Press, 1990.

Hildegard of Bingen's *Book of Divine Works with Letters and Songs,* ed. Matthew Fox. Bear &Co., 1987

Hildegard of Bingen: *Selected Writings,* trans. Mark Atherton. Penguin Classics, 2001.

Hutchinson, Gloria, Turning Pain into Power: A Retreat with Gerald Manley Hopkins and Hildegard of Bingen.

King-Lenzmeier, Anne *Hildegard of Bingen.* Liturgical Press, 2001.

Lachman, Barbara, *The Journal of Hildegard of Bingen*, a novel. Bell Tower, 1993.

Lachman, Barbara *Hildegard, The Last Year.* Shambala, 1997.

Mount, Toni, *Medieval*

Medicine; Its Mysteries and Science. Amberley, 2015.

Newman, Barbara, *Sister of Wisdom, St Hildegard's Theology of the Feminine.* Scolar Press, 1987.

Strehlow, Wighard Dr & Hertzka, Gottfried MD, *Hildegard of Bingen's Medicine.* Bear & Company, 1988.

Strehlow, Wighard Dr, *Hildegard of Bingen: Spiritual Remedies.* Healing Art Press, 2002.

Swanson, R.N., *The twelfth-century renaissance.* MUP, 1999.

Sweet, Victoria, *God's Hotel A Doctor, A Hospital, and a Pilgrimage to the Heart of Medicine.* Riverhead Books, 2012.

Uhlein, Gabriele OSF, *Meditations with Hildegard of Bingen.* Bear & Co., 1983.

Background Reading

Cadwallader, Robyn, *The Anchoress.* HarperCollins, 2016.

O'Connell, Mary, *The King's Daughter: Hildegard of Bingen, a Medieval Romance.* Handmaid Press, 2003.

O'Donohue, John, *Anam Cara.* HarperCollins, 1998.

Sacks, Oliver, *Migraine: Understanding a Common Disorder,* Long, 1985, Vintage, 1999.

Sharratt, Mary, *Illuminations: A novel of Hildegard von Bingen.* Mariner Books, 2012.

There are several informative websites: healthyhildegard.com, landderhildegard.de

Discography

Hildegard von Bingen: In Portrait. *Ordo Virtutum.* DVD. Opus Arte, 2003.

A Feather on the Breath of God: Sequences and Hymns by Abbess Hildegard of Bingen. *Gothic Voice,* dir. Christopher Page. Emma Kirkby (soprano) Hyperion DCA 66039, 1981.

Canticles of Ecstasy: Hildegard von Bingen, BMG Music, 1994.

Vision: The Music of Hildegard Von Bingen, CRMA, 1995.

Heavenly Revelations: Hildegard Von Bingen: Heavenly Revelations Hymns* Sequences* Antiphons* Responses. HNH International, 2001.

Liebe in Fulle: Lieder der Heiligen Hildegard: Gesungen von Keiko Sunohara Rupertsberg (Japanese)

www.ingramcontent.com/pod-product-compliance
Lightning Source LLC
Chambersburg PA
CBHW071812080526
44589CB00012B/763